DAMN!

DAMN!

A Cultural History of Swearing
in Modern America

ROB CHIRICO

FOREWORD BY KEITH ALLAN

PITCHSTONE PUBLISHING
Durham, North Carolina

Pitchstone Publishing
Durham, North Carolina 27705
www.pitchstonepublishing.com

Copyright © 2014 by Rob Chirico

To contact the publisher, please e-mail info@pitchstonepublishing.com

Printed in the United States of America

21 20 19 18 17 16 15 14   1 2 3 4 5

Library of Congress Cataloging-in-Publication Data

Chirico, Rob.
 Damn! : a cultural history of swearing in modern America / Rob Chirico ; Foreword
by Keith Allan.
     pages cm
 Includes bibliographical references and index.
 ISBN 978-1-939578-20-4 (pbk. : alk. paper)
 1. English language--United States—Obscene words—History. 2. English
language—United States--Obscene words. 3. English language—United States—
Swear words—History. 4. English language—United States—Swear words. 5.
Swearing—United States—History. 6. Americanisms—History. I. Title.
 PE3724.O3C45 2014
 394—dc23
                            2013049668

*"If my devils are to leave me, I am afraid
my angels will take flight as well."*
—Rainer Maria Rilke

"Life is a four-letter word."
—Lenny Bruce

CONTENTS

FOREWORD

Damn! A Cultural History of Swearing in Modern America is a highly entertaining, well-written, comprehensive, and instructive account of dysphemistic language in America. Much evidence is presented that what is offensive changes over time such that, today, religious terms and words for bodily effluvia and sexual acts are becoming or have already become more acceptable in public fora than are slurs against a person's race, gender, and mental or physical deviation from the norm. Thus one footballer insulting another with "You black cunt!" suffers greater disapproval for "black" than for "cunt."

Over millennia, attempts to stamp out swearing have met with little to no success. Censorship and repression, whether they amount to full-blown sanctions or merely social niceties, only ever provide a more fertile breeding ground for "dirty" words to thrive. One only has to look at the oxymoronic behavior of the Victorian middle classes in Britain: when sex ceased to be talked about openly, the sex trade and pornography flourished underground. Analogous is the failure of Prohibition to stamp out social drinking in the 1920s and the current failure of punitive drug laws to stamp out social drug use: instead both have strengthened organized crime syndicates to supply illicitly what people want. And people want to be able to use bad language on certain occasions.

Rob Chirico's book shows that genteel behavior is very superficial. It is a normal part of human behavior to swear and curse and be obscene, and if we hold the lid on it for much of our social life, there are always occasions when the lid comes off. There are many entertaining anecdotes in *Damn!* to illustrate the point. The reason, as Alan Read pointed out, is the "titillating thrill of scandalized perturbation." Swearing is often castigated as the language of the inarticulate, but there is absolutely no evidence for this blatant prejudice. There is some evidence that males may refrain from swearing in the company of female acquaintances, while females are more reticent about swearing in front of authority figures and family than before male friends and peers. Social swearing typically diminishes if there are nonswearers present, because shared swearing patterns indicate in-group membership.

Children of both sexes use swearwords from as young as one year old and the practice continues into old age—even when other critical linguistic abilities have been lost. People with certain kinds of dementia and/or aphasia can curse profusely, producing what sound like exclamatory interjections as an emotional reaction. However, when called upon to repeat the performance, they are unable to do so because they have lost the capacity to construct ordinary language. The explanation is that swear words are stored in a different location, or else accessed differently, from other vocabulary. This, too, may explain swearing as one manifestation of an emotionally disturbed state of mind.

Most cussing is an emotive reaction to anger or frustration, something unexpected and, usually, undesirable. This is the expletive function of swearing—the use of a swear word to let off steam. Even where used with an audience, such displays are autocathartic: the (unconscious) intention is to display a particular attitude or degree of feeling to oneself and anyone who happens to be in earshot.

An often ignored function of swearing is to spice up what is being said, to make it more vivid and memorable (e.g., "On the wall of his office was a framed Elbert Hubbard homily, If You Work For A Man, For Heaven's Sake Be Loyal To Him, blasphemously known to the apprentices as the bumsuckers' oath"). This may account for some of the obscenities that are the hallmark of chef and restaurateur Gordon Ramsay, who had a celebrated TV cooking series called *The F-Word*. Ramsay uses obscenities as discourse particles—where other people might use *like, well, I mean, you know*, and the like. Like other discourse particles, obscene expressions affect the way an utterance is understood.

Ramsey also abuses people with swear words. Such abuse includes curses, name-calling, and derogatory comment directed toward others to insult or wound them. Speakers also resort to swearwords to talk about the things that frustrate and annoy them, things that they disapprove of and wish to disparage, humiliate and degrade. To insult someone verbally is to abuse them by assailing them with contemptuous, perhaps insolent, language that picks on a person's physical appearance and mental ability, character, behavior, beliefs, and familial and social relations to degrade them. Thus insults are sourced in the target's supposed ugliness, skin color and/or complexion, over or undersize (too small, too short, too tall, too fat, too thin), perceived physical defects (squint, big nose, sagging breasts, deformed limb), slovenliness, dirtiness, smelliness, tartiness, stupidity, untruthfulness, and so forth.

We should not forget the use of swearing and insult as a mark of in-group solidarity, as illustrated in this 1920s *Punch* cartoon.

FIRST YOUTH: Hullo congenital idiot!
SECOND YOUTH: Hullo, you priceless old ass!
DAMSEL: I'd no idea you two knew each other so well!

Apparent insult becomes banter, teasing, sounding, playing the dozens (there are many other terms, too).

Iron is iron, and steel don't rust,
But your mama got a pussy like a Greyhound bus.

At best these involve a confrontation of wit, insight, and upmanship in which people try to outdo each other in the richness of their rhetorical scorn by taunting another person with insults about them or their family.

For the faint-hearted (or pure of lip) there are euphemistic dysphemisms that substitute would-be innocuous words for swear words: *shoot/sugar* for shit, *screw/fiddle-faddle* for *fuck*, *the C-word* for *cunt*, *gee* for *God/Jesus*, and a myriad more. Rob Chirico's *Damn!* expatiates on all the matters raised in this foreword and more. I wholeheartedly recommend it to the reader.

—**Keith Allan**
Sunshine Coast, Australia

INTRODUCTION

FRANKLY, MY DEAR, I DO GIVE A DAMN!

"In certain trying circumstances, urgent circumstances, desperate circumstances, profanity furnishes a relief denied even to prayer."
—Mark Twain

When Stephen Sondheim was writing the lyrics for "Gee, Officer Krupke," to be sung in the 1957 musical *West Side Story*, he was hoping to be the first person to use a serious four-letter obscenity in a Broadway show: "Gee, Officer Krupke—Fuck you!" This did not come to pass. Columbia records balked because obscenity laws would prohibit the recording from being shipped over state lines. In the end, the line was changed to "Krup you!"— Sondheim has since maintained that it may be the best lyric line in the show. Is there any doubt what the lyric would be if it were written today? In another line from the play, the character Tony sings "Something's Coming." Well, that something is here, and in full bloom: public swearing in America as it has never been heard before.

You may call it swearing, but others denounce it as profanity. Then again, perhaps your family warned against cursing or cussing as un-ladylike, un-gentlemanly, or simply rude. In school, teachers are more likely to condemn it as foul-mouth language, vulgarity, or downright "damnable" obscenity. If you went to Catholic school, taking the Lord's name in vain could have sent you on the highway to "hell"—a word in itself that was routinely censored from film and TV not so many decades ago. Were you chastised for regularly swearing a "blue streak" or spouting "potty-mouth" talk? Or were all of these "dirty words" just *fucking* bad language that might have resulted in threats of having your mouth washed out with soap? Except for a scene in Jean Shepherd's *Christmas Story*, I don't know if anyone has ever actually had his mouth washed out with soap for cussing, but if so, it evidently has not daunted Americans from openly cussing, cursing, and swearing like the dickens. And, there are times when the swearing goes right over our heads. Can you honestly say that you were so busy nervously sitting on the edge of your movie seat during a frantic car chase that you may not have even noticed the choice expletives belted out by the hero?

Prior to the 1960s, four-letter words were safely kept at bay by media censors, by prudent parents and teachers, and by a self-conscious monitoring of one's own language in the name of discretion. Then came a tumultuous decade. There was the Vietnam War with its unrelenting attack by protestors at home. Civil rights atrocities prompted nationwide demonstrations that resulted in solidarity and race riots. A sexual revolution embraced "free love" and spawned communal living, "swinging," and a healthy stream of books that told you how to do it all with vim and vigor. A president was assassinated. John Lennon incited the ire of hundreds of thousands of Americans with his comment that the Beatles were more popular than Jesus Christ, resulting in massive "Burn the Beatles" incidents around the country. Men's hair grew longer, and women's skirts got shorter. There were sit-ins, love-ins, be-ins, and Rowan and Martin's *Laugh-In*. Movies, music, and public discussion all challenged rights granted by the First Amendment. The result, as Timothy Jay concisely put it, was "to create less conservative and more open explicit means of communication." Taboo language that had once resided in discreet privacy was becoming public domain, and the forbidden four-letter words that had been reserved for a small and select group of places were soon openly in play almost everywhere.

The specific definitions for such terms as "swearing," "obscenity," and "profanity" will be touched upon later, but for our purposes, the words will be used interchangeably throughout this book. But whatever we want to call it, cursing or swearing, colorful and off-color language has peppered our English speech for as long as we can tell. Swearing is universal, and the reasons—or excuses—for it are as diverse as are the very words and phrases that we have all come to know, love, or excoriate. Nevertheless, until comparatively recently, broadcasting so-called dirty words over the air and dropping the "F-bomb" in polite, public conversation were apt to shock people, but that has all been dramatically changing right before our eyes—and ears. Listening to actors swearing at the Academy Awards, reading about vice presidents telling senators to "fuck" themselves, and watching television shows like *South Park* where cusswords are thrown about like confetti on New Year's Eve demonstrate that there is a "spreading effect" of an unceremonious loosening up of language that is altering the way we speak and think. Politics, the arts, economics, social and sexual relationships, and family interactions have all been touched by this greater latitude in speech.

Some may challenge that we are actually swearing more openly, although I doubt there are few in that camp. What is certain, however, is the "visibility" of swearing that was made possible through the enormity of our technological ability to disseminate practically everything we see and hear. With public and private video surveillance as common as mood stabilizers, and individuals playing James Bond and Weegee with their smart phones and iPads, every one of us has been more photographed or recorded than Marilyn Monroe. The recent spate of celebrities, newscasters, and our neighbors being caught mouthing something inappropriate proves that we should heed the cautious maxim, "Never assume that a gun is not loaded or that a microphone is turned off." Some may speculate that we swear more loudly and publicly because we live in a society that is more violent and angry than a few decades ago. These are many of the same people who are often prone to long for the chimerical "good old days." What is certain, though, is that technological intercommunication has made a good deal of what was once nestled safe and secure under the veil of privacy now open to the all-seeing public eye. To turn a phrase, "We have seen Big Brother—and he is us."

Timothy Jay in his *Cursing in America* appeared to be stating the obvious in 1992 when he noted that some venues especially inhibited dirty words and intensified their shock value. He mentioned church, television, stage, and the dining table. Nearly twenty years later it is arguable that the church is probably the last of those four places where cursing would truly be shocking, since television, stage, and even the dining room table no longer seem to rebuke it. Just pause for a moment and think about your own personal contact with cussing and consider the "F-bomb." Who goes a day without hearing it or, indeed, dropping it himself?

Just over the course of a few weeks in late 2013, New England Patriots quarterback Tom Brady dropped the "F-bomb" on national television after a loss; CNN's John Berman was caught saying it while coming back from a commercial break; the *Columbia Journalism Review* (CJR) printed it on its cover; and, according to the season's hottest political book, *Double Down: Game Change 2012* by Mark Halperin and John Heilemann, reported that the Obama administration uses it like "please" and "thank you."

What once would have scandalized most TV viewers or playgoers might now be greeted with annoyance or condescending disapproval at best. More likely, a dropped, well-positioned disreputable word or phrase in an appropriate situation will be greeted with complaisance if not assent. As for casual conversation, the word—or words—may even go unnoticed, as in the following interchange from the Cohn brothers *The Big Lebowski*:

> THE STRANGER: *"There's one thing, Dude. Do you have to use so many cusswords?"*
>
> THE DUDE: *"What the fuck are you talking about?"*

Profanity, once reserved for locker rooms, bars, pool halls, and the military—on and off the battlefield—was severely frowned upon right up through most of the last century. We had become so indoctrinated to the taboo of public swearing that when someone mentioned the phrase "four-letter words," it was not bloody likely that "foot," "shot," or "cook" would spring to mind. Even when stultified by dashes and asterisks, as "f***," "sh*t," and "c*ck," did they call to mind anything but "fuck," "shit," and "cock"? Edward Sagarin asserts that no other word in the English language could be so readily understood as "fuck." As he put it, "The monarch reigns over language." By contrast, erstwhile unprintable words are now emphatically spelled out in books; uttered throughout films and stand-up comedy acts; and have found new and inexhaustible life in our daily conversations via the Internet, Facebook, and Twitter. John Pareles, *New York Times* music critic, posed several suggestions that arrant swearing emerged out of post-World War II realism, demographic changes, bravado, freedom, permissiveness, the Beats, the 1960s, hip-hop, the decline of Western civilization, or all of them at once. Cussing in public has become more the rule than the exception, sometimes even on formal occasions.

True, cursing had a very bad beginning. But what originated as wishing harm on another person (as in very specific imprecations like "go to hell" or "God damn you") has developed into any number of expressions in which "cursing serves the emotional needs of the speaker." Once upon a more-cautious time, "darn" was a euphemism for "damn," "heck" for "hell," and "shoot" for "shit." Commenting on the latter, George Carlin made one of his many astute linguistic observations: everyone says "shit." "You can't fool me, 'shoot' is just 'shit' with two Os." When John Stewart is "blipped" on the *Daily Show*, I doubt that if anyone watching TV is puzzled as to what he just said. During the 2012 election campaign, he railed against *Fox News'* multifaceted spin on Mitt Romney's infamously ill-fated secret 47 percent video by reporting that there was "chaos on Bull-[blip] Mountain." I, for one, did not infer that he was referring to bullfinches, and "shoot" was right out of the question.

On the contrary, today hardly anyone says "shoot, "heck," or "darn," and there is probably an entire generation unfamiliar with that ludicrous euphemism "aw shucks." Those decidedly choice substitutions of just a few years ago have since lost their piquancy. Ashley Montagu, in his groundbreaking *The Anatomy of Swearing*, believed that the trend for the future use of four-letter words was unpromising. He maintained that with "the relaxation of the taboos in print, it is not long before they lose their power to frighten and annoy and are employed in open speech." He then predicted that as soon as four-letter words become acceptable Standard English, they would be weakened and might even disappear entirely from the swearer's vocabulary. While he was right on the money with his initial observation, thus far his prediction—made in 1962—is off by a long shot.

Even so, just as the profusion of such inoffensive demonstratives as "awesome" and "awful" has diminished their initial import, the casual overuse of profanity has caused it to lose its notorious shock. As a result of this overkill, we have become more insistent in our swearing and, as a result, we are continually upgrading to meatier concoctions like "fuckwad" and "abso-fucking-lutely," along with "fuck's" other endless variations, to bolster the diminishing power of the original word. But even "abso-fucking-lutely," technically called an integrated adjective or an "in-fix," when used casually in certain circles is neither shocking, nor even particularly attention getting (unless perhaps you utter it while suddenly spinning your head around 360-degrees, *Exorcist*-style, while spouting it amidst a shower of green-pea soup). What is pertinent here is that as much as the casual overuse of "damn" has gradually usurped its tame predecessor "darn," it no longer seems to have enough clout. Similarly, the stronger four-letter words that have replaced damn also seem to have diminishing returns, particularly when repeated throughout the course of one's speech.

One criticism against repetitive profanity is that it is the product of a lazy or sloppy vocabulary, and that we should invent new swear words to displace the shoddy old ones. Try as we earnestly seek to improve our swearing—or dismiss it entirely—it all takes time and great effort, neither of which is usually available when we swear the most: when something unexpectedly happens to us out of the blue, so to speak. Do you have the time to play Cyrano and pause for a moment to ponder, and then deliver a proper *bon mot* when you have just sliced off a bit of your forefinger along with the tomato you were cutting? Witticisms are hardly at hand when you are suddenly confronted with catastrophe. Batman's TV sidekick Robin was a master at this: "Holy strawberries Batman, we're in a jam!" Otherwise, unless you are entirely impassive and have a store of apt retorts at your disposal, like "Well, Roger me with a Siberian leek," you will be more likely to yelp your customary four-letter oath. Most emotional swearing is of the moment. Serious or banal, it is completely spontaneous. Whether that abrupt incursion into the status quo calls out for anger, fear, despair, or rebellion, *spontaneity* is the "mother" of universal emotional swearing. It is the objectification of the primordial howl—Whitman's sounding of the "barbaric YAWP over the roofs of the world." And like that YAWP, our volatile outburst cannot be a bit tamed, and it may indeed be untranslatable.

Emotional swearing is as common as high-fructose corn syrup. But unlike high-fructose corn syrup, which may just barely be seen in tiny print on the ingredient list of a bottle of catsup or a can of cola, swearing is right there in our face every day without any warning. Not to beat corn syrup to death—although it might be a good idea if only one could—its uses are seemingly boundless. In much the same way, swearing has a chameleon-like existence, and it stealthily creeps about in many guises. Apart from those negative instances already mentioned, we also can suddenly resort to all-encompassing F-word for elation and camaraderie. Whatever the choice of words or phrases, though, it is the context that is critical to their meaning. Ruth Wajnryb breaks down the context of swearing into three "broad domains of achievement" in which most swearing can be classified: catharsis, aggression, and social connection. Whether you've just smashed your thumb with a ball-peen hammer, or someone at the grocery store grabbed the last baguette from the shelf, or an old chum suddenly dropped by with an eighteen-year-old bottle of single malt Scotch, "son of a bitch" could be suitable for each of those ephemeral emotional responses. All three are different types of responses to different motivations, however. The latter two are expressed with clarity of judgment, while the first is a pure emotional, noncognitive response, rather like crying or laughing. Just because it sounds like language, doesn't mean it is. Just as it is with a spontaneous hearty guffaw after a good joke, that cuss of yours is basically an instinctive vocal reflex and not a direct verbal statement. To wit, linguist Steven Pinker explains that whereas genuine language is seated in the cerebral cortex, the hammer expletive is one of many "vocalizations other than language" that occur somewhere else. He goes on to say that these responses are not controlled by the cerebral cortex, which controls language, but by older neural structures in the brain stem, which is to say, subcortically: the amygdala made me do it!

No one is immune to this emotional outlet, not even babies. Not yet able to speak, infants express their emotions through crying, and their crying can grow exponentially as the situation demands it. Robert Graves was one of the earliest scholars to address swearing as a definite physiological function rooted early on in crying. He noted that as we grow, crying is discouraged as a signal of weakness, and, he added, "Silence under suffering is usually impossible. The nervous system demands some expression that does not affect towards cowardice and feebleness and, as a nervous stimulant in a crisis, swearing is unequalled. It is Saturnalian defiance of Destiny." Remember to quote Graves next time someone looks at you askance for swearing. And, if Graves won't do, try Nietzsche: "It also seems to me that the rudest word, the rudest letter, is more good-natured, more honest than silence. . . . All who remain silent are dyspeptic."

Regarding emotional swearing, you don't necessarily need to be angry or overjoyed to let fly a flurry of blistered epithets. Boredom is as real an emotion as any, and it has its hold on profanity just as any other passion might. Sometimes a cuss word may creep out merely because someone is so bored that there's nothing else to moan besides, "This shits." This takes us to a vital point: whatever the situation, swearing somehow functions as a conduit—it is a source of expedient release for a multitude of the most diverse emotions. Often when we swear we are figuratively and literally "giving vent to our anger." Some of us may readily "give vent," even if we are not paying the least bit of attention to the verb "to vent." George Bush Sr. certainly did not when he defended his much-criticized China policy by responding to reporters, "So, I'm glad you asked it because then I vented a spleen here." Despite his curious usage, Bush was on the right track. We rarely think of it, but verbally "venting" something is doing exactly that: venting and ventilation are means of clearing the air.

By the same token, swearing is a spontaneous system of ventilation for the swift eviction of any of those would-be psychological beasties that are momentarily plaguing us. In fact, much of our swearing is probably not directed at other people at all, but at our own predicaments as in solitary swearing. We need a verbal outlet whether we are merely slipping on the proverbial banana peel or holding on to our car steering wheel for dear life as we skid on a patch of ice at sixty miles per hour. Ironically, if you slip on that banana peel, and you find your outlet in swearing, your landing "ass over elbows" is just as likely to afford someone watching you an equally compelling, albeit diametrically opposed, outlet for another emotional response—laughter. The Germans have a word that everyone now seems to relish in: *schadenfreude*, the taking of joy in the misfortune of others. They would, wouldn't they?

Back to our three earlier examples for the use of "son of a bitch, of course the word "fucker" could just as easily have been substituted—in English, anyway. I qualify this because that all-too-familiar word "fuck," which is derived from the act of sexual intercourse, functions in English in ways that it does not in other languages. Europeans would never swear at an inanimate object, such as in "this fucking computer," using a literal translation of the sexually derived word "fucking," but there will be more on that in chapter 2. Suffice it to say for the moment, "fucking" is just for "fucking" in most other tongues. This is not to say that other languages do not have their own raunchy phraseology for expressing their unadorned emotions. Telling someone *krijg de pleuris* (catch tuberculosis) hardly has the pith of "fuck you" for us, but it just might result in a poke in the mouth in old Amsterdam. And so, although the words may be different, the offensive intent is the same. The severity of the words has less to do with the words themselves than the underlying emotional implications. Bill Bryson summed up the intriguing circular effect of swearing rather nicely: "Forbidden words are emotive because they are forbidden and they are forbidden because they are emotive."

Swearing can also be a very social affair, inspiring bonding in critical situations. One example, which we will particularly elaborate on later, is swearing in the military. It can also betray a social solidarity against authority, as may be heard in rap songs denouncing the brutality of the police, or the oppression imposed by government. Naturally, although we may all swear to some degree, we also swear by degree. One man's "fuck" is another man's "fudge." David Crystal acknowledged the universality of swearing in *The Cambridge Encyclopedia of the English Language*: "Everyone swears—though the mild expletive of sugar or golly by one person would probably not be considered swearing by someone whose normal imprecation is sonofabitch or motherfucker." Moreover, sometimes it just sounds so good. Just recall Whitman's "YAWP!" And, to quote Duke Ellington, "If it sounds good, it is good." A hip clothing outfitter out of San Diego apparently think it sounds good, as they call themselves Mudafuga.

Despite our need to swear, and our ability to do it most hysterically and histrionically at times, historically our society has preferred that we put a damper on that vent, and over the years it has set up watchdog groups to make certain that the vent stayed shut. Censorship predominated over the media and the arts of most of the twentieth century. Books were routinely banned by federal courts, and the movies were under the scrupulous eyes of groups like Hays Commission's Production Code, the Comstock Act, and the Catholic Church's Legion of Decency. To cite one of the most celebrated instances of a clash of words in Hollywood, one need only to look at the commotion stirred by the last line uttered by Rhett Butler in *Gone with the Wind*: "Frankly, my dear, I don't give a damn."

During the 1930s the Hollywood Motion Picture Production Code (MPPC) dictated what could not be shown or said on screen, and this included the word "damn." With a crucial finish line to an epic film on the line, some of the alternatives were suggested: "Frankly my dear, I just don't care," ". . . my indifference is boundless," and the ear-scalding, ". . . I don't give a hoot." Although legend persists that the Hays Office fined Selznick $5,000 for using the word "damn," in fact the Motion Picture Association board passed an amendment to the Production Code on November 1, 1939, to insure that Selznick would be in compliance with the code. Furthermore, saying that the words "hell" and "damn" would be banned except when their use "shall be essential and required for portrayal, in proper historical context, of any scene or dialogue based upon historical fact or folklore . . . or a quotation from a literary work, provided that no such use shall be permitted which is intrinsically objectionable or offends good taste." With that amendment, the MPPC had no further objection to the closing line. Ironically, Rhett Butler's brazen remark has gone on to be voted as the #1 movie quote of all time by the American Film Institute. There is even a video on YouTube that claims to be a collection of film's 100 greatest insults to date, appropriately concluding the foray with Butler's memorable phrase. As a historical aside, contrary to popular belief, this is not the first film to use the word "damn." The expletive was found in numerous silent intertitles and in several talkies, including *Cavalcade* (1933) and *Pygmalion* (1938).

The MPPC set censorship guidelines that governed the production of most United States motion pictures released by major studios from 1930 to as late as 1968. It spelled out what was acceptable and what was unacceptable content for motion pictures produced in the United States. Although most people still refer to it as the Hays Code after Will H. Hays, Joseph Breen took over from Hays in 1934, thus creating the Breen Office. Breen, the ruling czar at the office, was the man behind the kerfuffle over *Gone with the Wind*, and he was far more rigid in censoring films than Hays had been. The MPPC under him was so rigid that even the amusing 1946 fantasy *Angel on My Shoulder* was under attack for what would hardly raise an eyebrow today. The film, which starred Paul Muni as a vengeful convict, aided by Claude Rains as Satan, who comes back from the dead to kill a judge, was prevented from using such innocuous words as "jerk," "bum," and "sissy. The film did, however, manage to sneak in the line, "The Judge must be *screwy* or something!" [my italics] This all seems rather extreme when compared to the opening line of the 1987 film *House of Games*: "What the fuck!" And what would the MPPC have made of *Kick-Ass*, let alone *Kick-Ass 2*?

Up until and right into the 1960s, linguists acknowledged the proliferation of profanity, although they maintained that it still had its confines. Edward Sagarin, a pioneer in research on swearing, alleged, "Unutterable, the words can now be said, not only in the Army and Navy, among workers on the street, but even in polite and mixed company, *although not in a college classroom, or over radio, or on television*" [my italics]. Movies, television, and radio, however, were fairly modest operations that were far more controllable then compared to their modern-day reach. Cable networks, independent cinema, satellite radio programs, and the Internet were years and ideologies away. In some respects, the emergence of a nearly boundless media is much like what occurred at the concert in Woodstock: once the gates were down, there was no more collecting of tickets. Consider that the F-word was entirely absent from American cinema until 1970, and then look at the irreverent but revelatory 2005 film *Fuck: A Documentary*. The word is tossed about over 800 times, and that is not including its appearance in the film's graphics. As for a nondocumentary film, *The Wolf of Wall Street* leads the pack with an estimated 544–569 mentions. Meanwhile, the Internet Movie Database (IMDB) lists forty-six films with the word "fuck" in the title or subtitle, and Wikipedia has gone a step further, offering an "incomplete" list of some 200 films that make use of the word "fuck" or its variations at least 100 times. As to the herd of "hells" and "damns," apparently they stopped counting those sheepish words long ago, but I would not be surprised if their usage has been proportionately diminished in lieu of the thornier words that have replaced them.

Then there is the issue of the freedoms guaranteed by the First Amendment to the Constitution: "Congress shall make no law respecting an establishment of religion, or prohibiting the free exercise thereof; or abridging the freedom of speech, or of the press; or the right of the people peaceably to assemble, and to petition the Government for a redress of grievances." Indeed, the U.S. Supreme

Court has consistently held that speech may not be prohibited simply because some people may find it offensive. This has not prevented states from attempting to convict persons for alleged obscene language, even if most convictions are appealed to higher courts and eventually overturned. The result of testing the courts is that a new stage has been set, and everyone is getting into the act. The players range from the shock jockeys on the radio, and the "hey, I can't tell a joke without saying 'fuck' a hundred times" stand-up comedians, to *cinema verité* adherents, David Mamet, and all of those linguists attempting to make sense of the whole frenzied business. They are all out chewing up the scenery and spitting it out in four-letter words being beamed all over the planet in the now-axiomatic 24–7. In the words of Ira Gershwin (to the tune of Harold Arlen): "There is no let up the live long night or day."

Present-day commercial TV and movie ratings in general reflect this newer tide of leniency in the media. And yet it was just over forty years ago that the deservedly Oscar-winning 1969 film *Midnight Cowboy* was rated X in part for its use of "hard language" (it was since been re-rated as R). That hard language in *Midnight Cowboy*, and so many other films of the era, would be taken as mild cussing at best by our contemporary jaded standards. Just consider that *Meet the Fockers* and *Little Fockers* were both rated PG-13. It does not take Sherlockian deduction to glean that "Focker" is a tiny hop to "fucker," but bear in mind that, according to the MPAA, using "fuck" sexually will garner an R rating, but as a non-sexual epithet it receives the milder PG-13 rating. "Focker" as a sexual or non-sexual moniker would be in the mind of the prurient beholder: "nudge, nudge, wink wink." The films could have taken a more subtle family surname, albeit one with an equivalent jocular connotation, as in *Meet the Balls* or *Little Balls*, but the producers chose to go instead for the jugular on this one.

In another telling instance, Frank Zappa's Mothers of Invention released the vinyl album *We're Only in It for the Money* in 1967 with the strident but curious song "Mother People." It was curious in that, according to a parenthetical note in the song's printed lyrics, "the verse that really goes here has been censored out & recorded backwards in a special section at the end of side one." Following those directions, you heard, "Better look around before you say you don't care/ Shut your fucking mouth about the length of my hair/ How could you survive?/ If you were alive/ Shitty little person." This gimmick should have caused dismay much later in 1986 when the record came out on compact disc, because a CD cannot be played backward. There was no problem, however, since the verse was not censored, and you could listen to it where it had initially been intended. (In a further follow-up, the album has more recently been remastered for audiophiles, restoring the song and placing the backward line at the end—which, as was noted, cannot be reversed on a CD.)

For Frank Zappa and Mothers fans in the '60s it was a mischievous act of subversion to spin the disc backward, record the lines onto audiotape, and then reinsert the verse where it had been. By the '80s, the line was literally and figuratively not out of place in a culture growing immune to public swearing. Because of this influx of "fucks," albums had just begun to be labeled for "explicit lyrics" after pressure from the ever-vigilant Parents Music Resource Center (PMRC). With the surge of profanity in lyrics, the PMRC worked with the Recording Industry Association of America (RIAA) to standardize the label, creating the now-familiar black and white design: the "Tipper sticker," so named for Tipper Gore's participation in the PMRC. Regarding initials, the Internet is taking an opposite tact. In order to report on more brazen, shocking, or just adult material without chastisement, sites like the *Huffington Post* tag those headlines with the caveat: NSFW (not suitable for work).

As for television, one need only look at our most popular network shows, such as *Glee* and *30 Rock*, to see the shift in attitudes. Meanwhile, there is cable television and such shows as the animated *South Park*, which explodes with phrases like, "Hey, there, shitty-shitty fag-fag, shitty-shitty fag-fag, how do you do?" (to the tune of "Chitty Chitty Bang Bang"). Taking it to the limit, in one episode of South Park called "It Happens!" the word "shit" is uttered roughly once every eight seconds. Well, perhaps that was not the limit. When the gang hit the big screen in 1999 with *South Park: Bigger, Longer & Uncut*, a record 399 swear words garnered it the title of "Most Swearing in an Animated Film." Ironically, the raucous cartoon was about the good and bad that comes from swearing in the movies. So, one might even consider changing the erstwhile appellation "Silver Screen" to "Blue Screen."

We often hear of the "Me Generation." It may be a much looser term than "Baby Boomers" or "Generation X," but it is an effective indication of our need to show individuality in an indifferent world. It's our need to shout, "I'm mad as hell, and I'm not going to take it anymore," at the top of our lungs. And when we cannot shout it, we wear it. Another '60s phenomenon was the rise of the message T-shirt. Its inception may have begun quite innocently when the ubiquitous "smiley face" button was handed out at rock concerts, but it spawned a long line of slogan buttons, the most popular being "Make Love, Not War." The conservatives shot back with "Bomb Hanoi," and before anyone knew it, the youth of America, when not openly fulminating in public, all seemed to be wearing T-shirts shouting out everything imaginable for all to see and read.

Similarly, just as shirts prior to the '60s were mostly plain, it seemed that mostly unruly bikers and guys in the Navy sported tattoos. Then the ink hit the fan. People point to Janis Joplin's wristlet and small heart on her left breast, by the San Francisco tattoo artist Lyle Tuttle, as a seminal moment in the popular acceptance of tattoos as art. A 2006 a study done by the *Journal of the American Academy of Dermatology* found that 24 percent of Americans between 18 and 50 are tattooed—which is almost one in four—and that about 36 percent of Americans age 18 to 29 have at least one tattoo. Tattoo art is a lucrative business, even if one might speculate that a future equally lucrative business will be tattoo removal. Nevertheless, they evidence yet another need to express ourselves in repressive times. Ts, tats, and tirades: these are a cumulative representation of the modern-day American to retain his or her individuality while having his or her say. Visually or verbally, artistically or abusively, they are striving to make themselves and their ideas known; for they inherently know that anonymity is lethal. In the words of George Bernard Shaw from *The Devil's Disciple*, "The worst sin toward our fellow creatures is not to hate them, but to be indifferent to them: that's the essence of inhumanity."

With saltier language abounding, even the classics are not immune to verbal revisionism for greater impact. BBC radio broadcast a radio adaptation of *Wuthering Heights* in which Cathy and Heathcliff both utter the word "fuck." Writer and director Jonathan Holloway maintained that *Wuthering Heights* was a tragic tale of violent obsession and a tortuous unfulfilled relationship, warranting language as passionate as the story itself, and defended his position by asserting that his production was not a "Vaseline-lensed experience," and that he wanted to elbow out the idea that it's the greatest love story ever told. "It's not. The 'F' words are part of my attempt to shift the production to left field, and to help capture the shock that was associated with the original book when it was published." The playwright went on to argue that many adaptations of *Wuthering Heights* trivialize its content, and that an element of shock is integral to the book.

Those impugning the decision to air the word "fuck" protested that one change will lead to another and result in a contrarily libertine form of bowdlerism. Thomas Bowdler, an Edinburgh physician, unwittingly bequeathed us that term after he amended and sanitized the complete works of Shakespeare in 1818 in order to provide wholesome entertainment for the entire family. Keith Allan and Kate Burridge talk about the "guardians of linguistic goodness" in their splendid *Forbidden Words*. The fear among those opposed to the new *Wuthering*

Heights is that other productions will take Bowdler's approach in the opposite direction, and further adaptations of literary works will be verbally upgraded to suit our present penchant for swearing. And, as we have already mentioned, then what happens if the shock value of "fuck" goes completely south? Will the four-letter word need to be upgraded in some way to maintain the intensity of volatile situations?

At present, the United States is experiencing a linguistic, and therefore cultural, shift that is passively opening up to an amplified inclusion of profanity, or swearing, everywhere we turn, or turn away. Actors use it unceremoniously on the screen; rap singers revel in it; television is continually testing the Federal Communications Commission (FCC) with it. While Cole Porter himself never openly used them in his work, several of his songs were banned for being suggestive. He was most perceptive when he penned, "Good authors once too who once knew better words/ Now only use four-letter words/ Writing prose/ Anything goes." In something of a reverse on the chicken and egg analogy, it is not so much a question of which came first, personal profanity or media profanity, but which is affecting which the most. Is the media a reflection of our changing language, or are we becoming more inured to profanity by our constant confrontation with it in the media? Is the broad media an incentive for our profanity, or is it a reflection of it. Most likely it is a matter of mutual influences. It shapes our language while mirroring it. Naturally there are some exceptions that do not adhere to this broad supposition, such as swearing in the military and street talk, and they will be addressed in separate chapters. There are also neurological issues, such as Tourette Syndrome, which will be briefly touched upon, but they are pathological matters beyond the scope of this book.

Without any doubt, extensive mass communication in our society has obviated any dominant force that can regulate a complete level of control over what is heard or seen, as much as many local groups try: witness an article in a February 2011 article in the *New York Times* about a high school in Alabama that was awarded $5,000 for their efforts in establishing a no-cussing policy. This example of backlash is not isolated. James V. O'Conner, the founder of the Cuss Control Academy, avers that cussing has become an epidemic that has so totally infiltrated our daily lives that we are bombarded with it on the street, in shopping malls and schools, over the Internet, and even on hats and T-shirts. O'Conner has gone so far as to having penned the book *Cuss Control* to help those in dire need of cleaning up their vocabulary. You may not realize it, but even Google has a safety net, albeit a rather feeble one, in the search engine window on its toolbar. If you type in any number of four-letter words, it will not offer any suggestions. It will find everything you are looking for, and a hell of a lot more, once you hit enter, but you are on your own at the onset. This is yet another sound reason to learn how to spell correctly.

As much as O'Conner and the extracurricular anti-cussing clubs try, "you can't go home again" to the postulates of the past, whether they were good or bad, liberating or restricting. That said, the purpose here is not to be judgmental, but, rather investigative. For some individuals, swearing is a sign of bad manners, negative attitudes, or ignorance, while for others it is a healthy outlet and a signification of freedom. There should be an open-minded account of the genesis of open swearing and how the marked change in turn affected and continues to affect the language we speak and the culture in which we live. In the matter of a very short time, the course of so-called bad language's public veneer in an era when Columbia Records nixed the "fuck" from the *West Side Story* has evolved into the present-day leniency, when such an expletive is regularly articulated even in the most mundane of circumstances.

As one final example of this accelerated shift, even though J. D. Salinger had already used the "fuck" in his 1945 *Catcher in the Rye*, Norman Mailer was compelled to substitute the word "fug" for "fuck" in his 1948 novel *The Naked and the Dead* (which, as an aside, prompted Tallulah Bankhead to say upon first meeting Mailer, "So you're the man who can't spell 'fuck'"). Perhaps Mailer's work needs a revival on BBC Radio 3. Whether or not they were paying homage to Mailer, in the early 1960s Ed Sanders and Tuli Kupferberg named their band the Fugs, and they even had a thriving little Fugs Theater in New York's Greenwich Village. More recently, Reinhold Aman began publishing *Maledicta: The International Journal of Verbal Aggression*, a wildly witty periodical entirely dedicated to the scholarly study of foul language. Today you will find "fuck" not only in *Esquire*, *Playboy* and graphic novels, or in rock and rap music, but also in *Harper's*, *The New Yorker*, and *The Atlantic*. Although not yet fit to print in the *New York Times*, the salacious word "motherfuckers" was sung aloud from the stage of the Metropolitan Opera in February of 2011. This was all the while it was being simulcast over international radio, as well as in movie theaters in high definition, during John Adams's production of *Nixon in China*. And it wasn't even Dick Nixon who said it!

Yes, even with song, it has a long voyage since the sailing of the H.M.S. *Pinafore*:

Captain: Bad language or abuse, I never, never use, Whatever the emergency; Though "Bother it" I may occasionally say, I never use a big, big D

All: What, never?

Captain: No, never!

All: What, never?

Captain: Hardly ever!

All: Hardly ever swears a big, big D. Then give three cheers, and one cheer more, For the well-bred Captain of the Pinafore!

Damn!

So we commence with the question: whence, and what the "fuck"?

***

Editorial note: I would like to note that as much as this book is to focus on American English, ours is a "bastard tongue," and it will be inevitable to include examples from Great Britain and Australia when pertinent, as well as other European languages when a parallel is equally relevant.

1

WHAT'S IN A DIRTY WORD?

*Finally I was called as a witness in my own behalf. I took the stand
and Mr. Bendich examined me. Q. Mr. Bruce, Mr. Wollenberg yes-
terday said (to Dr. Gottlieb) specifically that you had said, "Eat it."
Did you say that?*

A. No, I never said that.

Q. What did you say, Mr. Bruce?

A. What did I say when?

Q. On the night of October fourth.

*MR. WOLLENBERG: There's no testimony that Mr. Wollenberg
said that Mr. Bruce said, "Eat it," the night of October fourth, if
your honor please.*

THE COURT: The question is: What did he say?

*THE WITNESS: I don't mean to be facetious. Mr. Wollenberg
said "Eat it." I said "Kiss it."*

*MR. BENDICH: Do you apprehend there is a significant difference
between the two phrases, Mr. Bruce?*

A. "Kissing it" and "eating it," yes, sir. Kissing my mother goodbye and eating my mother goodbye, there is a quantity of difference.

—Lenny Bruce, *How to Talk Dirty and Influence People*

If there was ever an example of a manipulation and exploitation of the context in which words were intentionally made to be confusing, that would be it. Taken out of context, both kiss and eat are entirely benign. We do them all the time, although we should probably be doing more of the former and less of the latter. Taken in context, Bruce's use of "kissing it" had the exact same intention as "eating it." In no way was the verb "kissing," as Bruce used it here, similar to the kissing he might bestow upon his mother. In fact, had it been a French court, "kissing it" would have been even more derogatory that "eating it" since the French use "baiser"—to kiss—as a correlative to our "fucking." Calling someone a "baiseur" is tantamount to us calling him a "fucker." Direct swearing in public was severely frowned upon in the late 1950s and early 1960s, and it was subject to fine or even imprisonment. Satirists like Bruce therefore often couched their expletives in careful substitution of double entendre. I say "often," because it was also Bruce's custom to shoot straight from the hip with unvarnished four-letter words—and longer. Whether it was his rants against government or his playful dissecting of words and phrases, I would go on to add that if there was one individual in the last hundred years who altered the way we speak in public, it was Lenny Bruce.

Thanks to his injudicious use of "cocksucker" or "tits and ass," Lenny Bruce was arrested half a dozen times and was banned outright from several U.S. cities. Throughout his career he playfully tested the limits of censorship. In one of his famous "bits," as he called them, he pointedly questioned the value of words in and of themselves: "You can't put tits and ass on the marquee. Why not? Because it's dirty and vulgar, that's why not. Titties are dirty and vulgar? Okay, we'll compromise.

How about Latin? *Gluteus maximus, pectoralis majors* nightly. That's alright, that's clean, ass with class, I'll buy it. **Clean to you, schmuck, but dirty to the Latins!**" Kenneth Tynan, Britain's leading drama critic at the time, hailed Bruce: "We are dealing with an impromptu prose poet, who trusts his audience so completely that he talks in public no less outrageously than he would in private. . . . Hate him or not, he is unique and must be seen. Tynan was an undaunted champion of free speech in his own right, and he is particularly remembered for chalking up the first instance of mentioning that notably opprobrious no-no on BBC television when he said, "I doubt if there are many rational people in this room to whom the word *fuck* is particularly diabolical or revolting."

Apparently the Australian government did not agree with Tynan's assessment of Lenny Bruce. At his first show in Sydney he took the stage and declared, "What a fucking wonderful audience." Bruce was arrested immediately and consequently banned from performing there. In 1964, after a six-month trial, presided over by three judges, he was sentenced to four months in a workhouse. Constantly hounded by authorities in his last years, he forged a crusade of freedom of speech rather than merely taking pleasure in offending with dirty words: "Take away the right to say 'fuck' and you take away the right to say 'fuck the government.'" As such, it would seem that freedom of speech is just fine as long as nobody is offended by it. Bruce died in 1966, but he was given a posthumous pardon for his convictions in the state of New York, the first in its history. For a man who sought out truth while saying the hitherto unsayable, his legacy is inestimable. Those counted as having been influenced by him are far too numerous to list, but they include: Richard Pryor, Whoopi Goldberg, Jerry Seinfeld, Lewis Black, Sarah Silverman, Robin Williams, Bill Maher, Sam Kinison, Eddie Izzard, Howard Stern, and, of course, George "shit, piss, fuck, cunt, cocksucker, motherfucker, and tits" Carlin. We may even take it as homage to Lenny Bruce that Carlin culled his little group from a monologue by Bruce. Lenny was, in a word, the "precursor" to the swearing on stage that we take for granted today. Ironically, as an aside, it was Carlin's list of just-mentioned "heavy seven" words that went on to become the de facto standard for FCC rulings on what could indeed not be said over the public airwaves. Thanks, George!

Lenny Bruce may have appeared before judges in court, but he also appeared at Carnegie Hall. As did George Carlin. And not only did Carlin appear, he thoroughly entertained everyone—or, we think everyone, because there were no police officers lying in wait there to arrest him for uttering a deemed "obscenity" like "cocksucker." Carlin went far beyond the taboos imposed upon Bruce, and he flaunted them—at substantial ticket prices, and with nary a slap on the wrist. But Carlin knew his audience. He knew that they had been liberated by the daring voice of Lenny Bruce and were now ready to sit back and enjoy every savory verbal vice that had been hitherto restricted. Carlin, in his raised-brow, mock-ignorant voice during one of his performances asked the audience about the word "cocktail." Looking around the room, he slowly and melodiously chirped, "What is that?" Then, after the famous Carlin pause he resumed, "Cocktail. Yeah. Women want cock; men want tail." The audience lapped it up. Bruce would have loved it, too; but he would have had his ass in a sling if he said it in any one of the hundreds of places that Carlin said it.

Bill Maher went on to praise Bruce when he said, "A lot of people can be funny—he was brave." And he also acknowledged Bruce's accomplishment as a champion of freedom of speech because comedians and satirists such as himself could now go anywhere in the United States and say whatever they wanted. David Skover, Fredric C. Tausend Professor of Law at the Seattle University School of Law and author of *The Trials of Lenny Bruce*, teaches, writes, and lectures in the fields of federal constitutional law, federal courts, free speech, and the Internet. For Mr. Skover, "Lenny created the freest free speech zone in America." He lamented that Bruce's life was also a story of the First

Amendment: it was "the story of a free speech martyr." Intermittently funny and serious as he was, Lenny single-handedly changed stand-up comedy and, consequently, the public's receptivity to verbal taboos. In the words of Steve Earle from his song "F The CC," "Just don't forget your history, dirty Lenny died so we could all be free."

Still, it wasn't until 1970, four years after Bruce's death, that the first "fuck" was uttered in a major American motion picture. The film was *M*A*S*H*. While lined up in the memorable football sequence, the character "Painless" Potter snarls at an opponent, "All right, bub, your fuckin' head is comin' right off." (The first major, albeit now-forgotten, British film to feature the expletive was *I'll Never Forget What's name* in 1967. It was charmingly uttered by the always charming Marianne Faithful: "Get out of here, you fucking bastard!") Back then that line from *M*A*S*H* probably produced the biggest single laugh of the film. It was like the first pie in the face or slip on a banana peel. Nobody expected it. At the right moment, the carefully chosen instance can still generate a laugh from the word, but it won't have any of the same impact unless the situation in which it is employed is just as unexpected.

Robert Redford's muffled "Oh shit!" was greeted with a similar response the previous year in *Butch Cassidy and the Sundance Kid*. Meanwhile, although *Meet the Fockers* set box office records after its 2004 release, the joke of saying "Focker" was wearing so thin by the time *Little Fockers* appeared in 2010, that it needed overkill to continue to produce a laugh. It was almost like watching an entire film devoted to someone slipping on a banana peel in new ways. Whether visual or verbal, a familiar gag loses its punch unless it is reinvented, and that is precisely what the movie *The Aristocrats* showed in 2005. *The Aristocrats*, which Netflix categorizes as a Social and Cultural Documentary, presents more than 100 stand-up comedians—some of whom are mentioned earlier in this chapter—telling the same raunchy joke in ways that would have had Lenny Bruce drawn, quartered, and then burned at the stake in his day. A lot happened in a mere forty-odd years that changed our public attitude toward talking dirty, whether influencing people or not.

My own first brush with the new indulgence of public swearing came in the early 1990s. I was living in Buenos Aires and teaching an art appreciation course to eight-graders at the American School. While approaching the reference desk in the library I overheard two Korean lads, obviously new to the English language, conversing. I paid little mind to their discourse until one of them casually blurted out, "That suck. That really suck!" As a boy who grew up in New York City, "suck," or more accurately, "sucks," in the above context, was a definite public no-no. It was hardly much more acceptable than "cunt" or even "fuck." In fact, as a verb, "suck" was very close to "fuck" in that it, too, was still notably rooted in sexual activities then. Naturally, I thought, these nonnative speakers had picked up the phrase without knowing its gravity, just as they had not grasped the subject-verb agreement. While hardly a prude, I thought it best to enlighten the fellows, and I mentioned to the young librarian behind the desk that he might want to point out that the phrase they were using was socially unacceptable. I skipped the fact that it was also grammatically incorrect. This time I was the one who was greeted with surprise. "Which phrase?" he asked. Looking around, I repeated it in a low voice. Looking at me as if I were dressed in the severe, black, button-down garb of the chap on a package of Quaker Oats, he replied, "Don't you watch *The Simpsons?*"

Let us rewind the clock a mere decade to the early 1980s when I watched the Elliot Gould film *Getting Straight* on late-night television. During the opening scene, the students on the staircase of a college are tossing an apple to one another, and laughing as they look at its front and back. The audience finally gets a glimpse of one side. Carved into the apple are the words, "There is no gravity." Having seen the film in the theater some years before, I recalled that when it was finally tossed to Gould, he laughs as he flips it around to read, "The Earth sucks." Except, on TV, you were not shown why he laughed—the scene revealing the lewd phrase was cut, leaving the TV audience at a loss to this now literally private joke. Other films were notable for their substitutions. The television audience watching the edited version of *Repo Man* (1984) did not hear the word "motherfucker," but heard, to my mind, the far more ingenious, and rather mellifluous, "melon farmer." Another head-scratching moment came when the line, "Hand me my keys, you fucking cocksucker," was changed on television to, "Hand me my keys, you fairy godmother," in the *Usual Suspects* (1995). Perhaps the most famous of all TV edits was in *Die Hard* (1988), when the character John McClane, played by Bruce Willis, trumpeted his immortal, "Yippee-ki-yay, motherfucker!" That enraged cry was toned down to the almost obsequious, "Yippee-ki-yay, Mr. Falcon."

Fast-forward to the present, where the word "suck" on television has become practically innocuous. Frequent use over time has stripped away the original wicked connotation. "Suck" is a variable, and language is often obscure in its own right or wrong. How is it that we can have a "blunt and cutting remark" when the adjectives are opposites? We do our best to make the colorful and descriptive most of a situation while being entirely confusing linguistically in the process.

For censorship, it would seem that context was, and still is, the key. In "It Hits the Fan," the 66th episode of *South Park*, the character Kyle has tickets to go to *The Lion King on Ice*, but another character, Cartman, tells him that the fictional HBC network's crime show *Cop Drama* is going to use the word "shit." This crime show leads to an outbreak of the word, resulting in a casual conversational use of the word by everyone in all walks of life; it is even invoked in schools. In a reference, if not a slam, to the confusing standards of indecency of the actual FCC, eventually, one Ms. Choksondik (a droll name in itself that would have been exorcised from TV in the past) is forced to clarify the acceptable context of the word to her students: the word is acceptable as a noun or adjective meaning bad or as an exclamation of disappointment. However, as a noun or adjective referring to feces, it is apparently unacceptable. The result completely confused the class—much as the FCC has confused all of us with its inscrutable rulings. It is difficult to take something out of context when the very ground of context is as firm as a puddle of mercury.

When national premium cable television began, it was a true upstart. Although HBO had a viewership of only a few thousand when first launched in the early 1970s, commercial network television was not oblivious to the potential that independent channels might have, and they were already in a panic. A mass campaign was organized in conjunction with the film industry to scare movie viewers into thinking that all TV would be pay TV. The cable stations played David with his sling to commercial television's sword-wielding Goliath and did not relent. In effect, they told the Big Three to "Go fuck themselves." Is it any wonder that over the years that cable, and then satellite TV, neither of which is bound by the same restrictions the FCC can impose upon network television, should brandish their rebel status? Furthermore, they did not have fickle or short-sighted advertisers to answer to.

Working on the belief that what had been holding television back was not the viewer, but the sponsor, the HBO stratagem was obvious: show uncut, commercial-free movies for a fee. They had figured out that the approach followed by broadcast networks—trying to please the sponsor and the audience—was a no-win situation. Instead, HBO began producing quality programming for a select audience that would pay a premium for it. That initial small audience has expanded to over 30 million viewers. As the lowly intruder grew to be a giant industry in its own right, with subscribers flocking to the fold, more cable stations emerged, and, it's fair to say, more diverse, quality programming appeared. Individual stations flaunted their spunkiness, their nonconformity, and their profanity in the face of noncable commercial TV. Premium cable shows like *The Wire, The Sopranos, Six Feet Under, Mad Men*, and *Boardwalk Empire*, among so many more, have been giving the major networks a run for their money. AMC and other basic cable stations share this freedom, but, as they are monitored by their sponsors, they tend to shy away from profanity.

The Big Three, soon to be joined by FOX, countered with the saucy adult-oriented *Desperate Housewives*, *30 Rock*, *NYPD Blue*, and *Glee*—all of which have attempted to take network standards to their limit, which is not very far by comparison with cable. Whether it's harsh reality or epic fantasy, you can bet your midnight special or your crossbow that expletives will be discharged at will on premium cable. Regarding the latter, there is an online video titled "Game of Fucks: 126 Reasons Why Game of Thrones Would Never Work on Basic Cable," which splices together every profanity uttered in HBO's popular *Game of Thrones* first two seasons in rapid-fire fashion. As you might well imagine, there are plenty of "bastards" (not just directed at the character and actual bastard Jon Snow), "whores," "cunts," and pretty much everything in between. I personally did not count them, but I will take them at their word that there are 126.

Attempting to keep TV wholesome, President George W. Bush signed the Broadcast Decency Enforcement Act of 2005 into law. As such, the maximum fine the FCC could impose per indecency violation increased tenfold, from $32,500 to $325,000, forcing network TV to tread more cautiously in its attempt to compete with cable and satellite. To understand the consequences network TV would incur if it aired an unedited premium cable channel show, take, for example, HBO's *Deadwood*—with its aptly named, and historically accurate at that, foul-mouthed saloon-owner Al Swearengen. Thanks to diligent followers of foul-mouthing, we know that the first show alone contained the following:

"fucks"—49

"cocksucker"—8

"shit"—7

"cunt"—3

"pissing"—2

"motherfucker"—1

There was only one "bastard." Perhaps it was too tame. Still, if any single network TV episode would dare try to emulate the use of profanity that was spouted in *Deadwood*, which over three seasons aired a cumulative 2,930 "fucks," the fine imposed upon that commercial network would be a whopping $95,225,000. And that does not include any of the other banned words. One wonders how much the FCC is scrutinizing network television for decency or for a chance to pocket some easy money.

The network television screen, though, is a very fragile barrier—the final media frontier? It is also a barrier that film and stage have already torn down, but television is slowly picking away at it. In one episode of *30 Rock*, the cast impishly, and impiously, reminisced about a bygone era when you could not say particular words on TV. They then went to enumerate many of those words, concluding with a hearty laugh about a time when you were not permitted to say such a thing as "ass wipe" on the air. Just think, this was the same medium that dictated in 1952 that Lucille Ball was "expecting" and not "pregnant." In effect, the *30 Rock* repartee was a both sly reveling in the freedom from more repressed times and a calculated testing of the waters to what they could get away with. Furthermore, the conversation was somewhere between Lenny Bruce's bold recitations of dirty words and George Carlin's glib repetition of the "heavy seven," straddling the once verboten and the greater permissiveness yet to come. Steven Bochco, creator of *NYPD Blue*, actually negotiated with his network over how many expletives could be used per episode. The arbitration must have been like buying a used car: Forty? No, thirty? Thirty-six? No, thirty-one. Eventually they agreed upon a head-scratching thirty-four, but you can bet your boots that the ante in the broader swearing game of network television will be going up every season.

But the game isn't over. On June 21, 2012, the Supreme Court declined to address whether the government still had the authority to regulate indecency on broadcast television, but excused two broadcasters from potential fines for several past violations of rules against cursing and nudity. In the words of Justice Anthony Kennedy, "The commission failed to give Fox or ABC fair notice prior to broadcasts in question that fleeting expletives and momentary nudity could be found indecent." With matters still up in the air waves, we must wait to see which court the ball will land in next.

2

WHAT'S SEX GOT TO DO WITH IT?

"You fucking fuck, fuck you!"
—Dennis Hopper from *Blue Velvet* (1986)

Although we may use the words "swearing" or "cursing" interchangeably on a daily basis, the specific definitions have been crucial for settling obscenity cases and deciding if someone should be fined for inappropriate usage. Take, for example, the incident of L.A. Laker's basketball star Kobe Bryant shouting a "homophobic slur" at a referee. The offensive slur in question was "fucking faggot," but Bryant was not fined $100,000—"Trump change" for him—for "fucking" as much as it was for saying "faggot." While "fucks" are shot and rebounded with swift regularity through every game, since they are never taken sexually, nobody calls fouls. In fact it was in basketball where the earliest mention of a slur hurled at a referee is recorded. It dates back to the end of the nineteenth century when a young woman playing at a Y.M.C.A in Springfield, Massachusetts, called James Naismith, the game's purported inventor, a "son of a bitch" after he charged her with a foul. As the shocked Naismith demurely put it, "She questioned my ancestry."

Although one can hardly believe that she was indeed questioning his lineage, "faggot" still has a very definite relation to sexual preferences—whether or not Bryant meant it as such, which, like our young miss, he probably did not. The Human Rights Campaign issued the statement, "Hopefully Mr. Bryant will recognize that as a person with such fame and influence, the use of such language not only offends millions of LGBT (lesbian, gay, bisexual, transgender) people around the world, but also perpetuates a culture of discrimination and hate that all of us, most notably Mr. Bryant, should be working to eradicate." Remember, though, that it was "faggot" and not "fuck" that raised the ruckus. For all of its heinous behavior in the past, "fuck" is getting a steady free pass these days as not necessarily being an obscenity. We will return to this oddity momentarily, but in order to understand why words are considered more offensive in one context over another, here is a brief glossary of some of the terms for swearing in their primary definitions in *Webster's Third International Dictionary*:

> **curse** (*n*): a calling to a deity to visit evil on one : a solemn pronouncement or invoking of doom or great evil on one : an imprecation for harm.
>
> (e.g.: May the gods take away your TV remote control, and that you should be electrocuted and go to hell while trying to change channels manually!)
>
> **curse** (*vb*): to rail at typically impiously and profanely : BLASPHEME.
>
> (e.g.: Damn you, goddamnit!)
>
> **profane** (*vb*): to violate or treat with abuse, irreverence, obloquy, or contempt (something sacred) : treat as not sacred.
>
> (e.g.: God is dead. But don't worry; Mary is pregnant again.)

profane (*adj*): unconcerned with that which is religious or with purpose of religion : not devoted to the sacred and the holy : SECULAR.

(e.g.: Let priests marry; it will give them a working description of hell.)

obscene (*adj*): disgusting to the senses usu. because of some filthy, grotesque, or unnatural quality.

(e.g.: May you be fucked by a donkey and be forced to keep its offspring and raise the little ass by yourself!)

vulgar (*adj*): generally used applied, or accepted : found in ordinary practice.

(e.g.: Wassup?)

As for "vulgar," it is not until you read far down into usage number 5b that you come upon: "lewd, obscene, or profane in expression or behavior." A man of the world with a most fitting surname, Captain Frances Grose straddled the two meanings in his application of it for the title of his 1785 *Classical Dictionary of the Vulgar Tongue*. Indeed, the distinction between profanity and obscenity has become clouded in English, and will most likely not be clarified—in English, that is. The designers of Esperanto took the older, more pedantic approach in an attempt to qualify the meanings of each word. Profanity in Esperanto is called "sakro," after the older French *sacre*, and consists of what English speakers would call "oaths": religious or impious references used as interjections. Obscenity in Esperanto is called "maldeca" (indecent) or "tabua" (taboo). These are the Esperanto words that refer to sexual acts, phrases, and bodily functions in nonclinical ways.

So, is "fuck" a curse, a profanity, an obscenity, a vulgarity, or all of the above? Legally, it has been charged with the first three over the years, whereas "vulgar" is just too loose a concept to render disciplinary action. As for us, the answer may depend on the context, but the F-word certainly fits the definition of the first sense of vulgar, the language of the common person.

Opting for "all of the above" would be the most fitting answer because of the multitude of meanings and intentions encapsulated in that single word. Love, hate, sex, war, religion, among so many other topics, have had volumes devoted to their subjective natures. As ideological concepts, perceivable phenomena, or philosophical reflection, it would be impossible to choose which of these subjects has engendered more speculation. Then there are words, pure and simple. If there ever was a simple word, though not so pure, that has had more written about it in English than any other, it is most decidedly "fuck." Discussed strictly as a word, "fuck," and its derivatives, is the hands-down winner. No other single word has had more ink spilled over its glories and diversities. On the heels of Lenny Bruce and his improprieties, George Carlin virtually narrowed down the source for almost all swearing in his "Seven Words That You Can Never Say on Television": shit, piss, fuck, cunt, cocksucker, motherfucker, and tits. But as exponential as each of these words can be in deference to swearing, each word is still more often linked to its original meaning than "fuck" is. "Fuck" is by far the most abstract. And more often than not, "fucking" is just an introductory enhancer to another more substantive idea: "that fucking ambulance chaser."

Although Melissa Mohr in *Holy Shit* rightly maintains that the "strongest offensive words can almost always be used nonliterally," taken by themselves as words, "piss" and "shit," tend to conjure up two very specific doings, while "fuck" alone is all over the place in ways that have nothing to do with "fucking." This is not to say that the other words are used only denotatively—or literally. Calling someone a "pisser" does not mean that the fellow is given to frequent urination, or that he has a "shitty" car refers to the fact that it is covered in bird turds. Similarly, saying that your computer is filled with cookies will not be construed as an invitation to drop by and have a snack of Chips Ahoy. The mind is astute enough to immediately determine the intended meaning of language without lingering over the evaluation of every possible image. Connotatively, or not given to anything specific, the words do have various and sundry applications. "Fuck" on the other hand is the basis for a nearly limitless exploitation of expressions. To illustrate the flexibility of the word, Geoffrey Hughes created a neat little chart of eight categories in which the most common swear words might be used:

1. *Personal:* '*You* ----!'"

2. *Personal by reference:* '*The* ----!'"

3. *Destinational:* '---- *off!*'

4. *Cursing:* '---- *you!*'

5. *General expletive of anger, annoyance, frustration:* '----!'

6. *Explicit expletive of anger, annoyance, frustration:* '---- *it!*'

7. *Capacity for adjectival extension:* '----*ing*' or ----*y*'

8. *Verbal usage:* '*to* ---- *about.*'

Among the words he enumerates, he includes the usual suspects—"damn," "fuck," "cunt," "shit," "fart," "piss," "bugger," "bastard," and "asshole," but only two can fulfill all eight modes: "fuck" and "bugger." Americans do not employ "bugger" in the same way that the British do, but for all intents and purposes, "bugger" is just a British euphemism for "fuck." (Sod—referring to sodomy—and shag share company with bugger across the pond, but are simply lawn material and rugs or bad haircuts here.) In American English, "fuck" stands alone.

Plenty has been penned about the history, derivation, and usage of the word, including a raucous little volume devoted solely to practically every sense of the word's usage, *The F Word* by Jesse Sheidlower. And an entire film has also been devoted to illuminating "fuck" and its vagaries, *Fuck: A Documentary*. It is Montagu's "monarch" of all curse words—so there is no need to rehash what can easily be referenced elsewhere. Nevertheless, there is one aspect of it that while mentioned is mostly glossed over: in English, at least, "fuck" is the most mercurial of swear words because it has escaped and run from the confines of its sexual root. Carlin's other words carry with them at least a glimmer of their scatological or sexual ancestry, but "fuck" is a lone wolf that can roam bawdily through its sexual home turf or wander far afield into uncharted linguistic lands. To reiterate, though, this is almost exclusively in English. While every other European language has its own word for "fuck," English appears to be unique in a more universal application. Let's take the following joke as an example:

> *In Jerusalem, a female journalist heard about a very old Jewish man who had been going to the Western Wall to pray, twice a day, every day, for a long, long time. So she went to check it out. She went to the Western Wall, and there he was! She watched him pray, and after about forty-five minutes, when he turned to leave, she approached him for an interview.*
>
> *"I'm Rebecca Smith from CNN. Sir, how long have you been coming to the Western Wall and praying?*
>
> *"For about fifty years."*
>
> *"Fifty years! That's amazing! What do you pray for?"*
>
> *"I pray for peace between the Jews and the Arabs. I pray for all hatred to stop, and I pray for our children to grow up in safety and friendship."*
>
> *"How do you feel after doing this for fifty years?*
>
> *"Like I'm talking to a fucking wall."*

To understand the uniqueness of this joke in English, try literally translating it into any other European language. The punch line would make no sense to a Frenchman. Although he does have a respective—or dis-respective—verb "foutre" and the milder "baiser," he would wonder why someone is referring to intercourse with a wall. "That fucking wall" would be something along the lines of "*cette putain de mur*" in French, or "that whore of a wall," and Spanish would be similar. The French are also quite enamored of shit—"*vous me faites chier*," which literally means "you make me shit," but implies that "you bore me." The sacrosanct "fucking" is reserved for, well, "fucking." But our English "fuck" is making inroads. Just as the Chinese will line up for MacDonald's (with rice) in Beijing and Palestinians will spend $27 for a bucket of soggy fries and limp chicken from Kentucky Fried Chicken smuggled across the border from Gaza into Egypt, our language has infiltrated other lands. The French have our *weekend* and *parking* in their Franglais, and *stress* and *snob* have passed into Anglitaliano. Our words continue—do I dare say—to enliven other languages without any reference to their own vocabulary. Similarly, we are seeing "fucking" this or that in other languages—except that it is exactly our English word that is appearing in lieu of the native version. This is more common in countries where English is a second language, such as the Netherlands or Norway. If you watch an episode of *Lilyhammer*, you will hear a character speak an entire diatribe in Norwegian, save for the English adjective "fucking." Very recently the Dutch have purloined our precious "fucking" as seen in *Hou je fokking bek* (Shut your fucking beak!). I say purloined because the actual word for "fuck" in Dutch is *neuken* and not *fokken*, or whatever. (I think the latter was sort of a German tri-plane, but I'm not betting on it.) Have we started another export trend?

While fuck's nonsexual use as an adjective, noun, verb, or adverb in English is omnipresent, it is simply absent from other tongues as such. Sarah Miles takes our usage to an ironic extreme as she blithely comments on the joys of nature in *White Mischief* (1987): "Another fucking beautiful day." Interestingly, the HBO series *Deadwood* fills its characters mouths with swearing. As to its authenticity in the 1880s, Sheidlower agrees with creator David Milch that the F-word was in use back then. But he says most of the nonsexual uses of it—as an intensifier, for example—didn't come about until around World War I. Milch's rationale, however, is that contemporary slurs are now quaint, and if you put a word like "goldarn" into the mouths of the characters, they would all wind up sounding like Yosemite Sam. Sheidlower has added that the mainstream use of the word has accelerated because open discussions of sexual matters are no longer as taboo as they once were. Thus everything connected to this, including nonsexual uses of sexual terms, becomes increasingly acceptable.

Then there are the cultures that seemingly have no swear words. As for the Japanese, Polynesians, Inuit, and American Indians, they are all said to be people who do not swear—which is to say that they do not have our manner of cusswords, per se. It does not, however, mean that they do not get angry if you spill sake on someone's antique Aka carpet, and insult you for having done so. If you doubt that there is any dearth of Japanese rancor, try watching some Japanese anime until your ears turn red. *Baka* literally means "idiot," but it is becoming a more offensive slur as public irritability increases in Japan. Language is also an embodiment of the culture in which it is spoken. If there are no swear words similar to ours in the Inuit's vocabulary, other words that are common, if not essential, to English are also completely absent. Imagine how difficult it was for the Christian missionaries to convert a race that did not have words for "sin" or "virgin." Nevertheless, for the hundreds of insults or compliments that you will dredge up from any of these tongues, you will not find one that directly corresponds to our sexually rooted "fuck" and meanders into countless other directions. And when it comes to "fuck off," there is nothing that comes close— even in English. To illustrate the asexuality of "fuck," we turn to this salty morsel:

A man is talking to his friend about a girl he met the night before.

"I went to the fucking pub and saw this fucking beautiful girl. I thought, 'Fucking hell, she's fucking gorgeous.'"

"What happened then?" asks his friend.

"I bought her a fucking drink and started fucking talking to her," he says.

"What happened then?" asks his friend again.

"She said she wanted to leave, so we tried to get a fucking cab but fucking ended up walking all the way to her fucking flat. Then she asked me in for a fucking drink."

"What happened then?"

"We made love."

(As we will see in the chapter on the military, this joke seems to have been popular with American soldiers during the Second World War. The difference is that by the time it reached civilian life in Britain, it seemed to have an off-handedness and not the coarseness, if not vulgarity, of the original.)

Without elaborating on this anomaly, Bill Bryson did find it odd that "fuck" was also used as a general expletive for anger: "It is a strange and little-noted idiosyncrasy of our tongue that when we wish to express extreme fury we entreat the object of our rage to undertake an anatomical impossibility or, still, to engage in the one activity that is bound to give him more pleasure than anything else." Other sources would agree with the remarkable singularity of our word. Timothy Jay's article "Do Offensive Words Harm People?" is predominantly about the legal issue of swearing and the necessity to have an understanding of context before passing judgment, since any attempts to censor words on a universal basis amounts to a violation of our First Amendment free speech rights. But as a noteworthy aside, he cites the lawyer C. Fairman, who examined the inconsistencies on the interpretation of "fuck" and demonstrated that many of the modern uses of "fuck" were divorced from the word's earlier predominantly sexual denotation. In turn, he adds, "Public swearing data indicate that the predominant use of fuck is to express emotional connotation (e.g., frustration, surprise) and not literal sexual denotation."

Among others, David Crystal has evaluated the symbolism and import that sound alone may have upon words. He maintained that when it comes to swearing, gentle sounds such as long vowels and nasal sounds along the lines of "meem" and "rahl" will hardly induce rancor however viciously you spew them compared to the sounds made by articulating "gack" or "krot." Monty Python's *Flying Circus* took a humorous approach to this in their "Woody and Tinny" sketch from episode forty-two. After disparaging tinny words like "litter bin" and "antelope," Graham Chapman delineates the difference between tinny and woody words and at one point lapses into a harangue: "No, no, the word, 'intercourse'—good and woody . . . inter. . .course . . . pert . . . pert thigh . . . botty, botty, botty . . . *(at this point his wife leaves the room)* . . . erogenous . . . zone . . . concubine . . . erogenous zone! Loose woman . . . erogenous zone . . . *(the wife returns and throws a bucket of water over him)* Oh thank you, dear . . . you know, it's a funny thing, dear . . . all the naughty words sound woody." In Crystal's long list of offensive words, he cites "chink," "dick," "cunt," "prick," "bloody," and, of course, "fuck." In effect, it is the sound that drives the word. He adds, "Indeed, if we look closely at the swearing formulae, we may find no meaning at all: *fucking hell* and other such phrases are literally nonsense." As an exercise, quickly speak aloud the following: "asterisk," "prickly pear," "continued later," and "cock-a-doodle-doo." Then say "ass," "prick," "cunt," and "cock." Similar sounds—different effect, no?

This departure from the literal nonsexual denotation is nothing new for the English speaker. Poring over Jesse Sheidlower's encyclopedic *The F Word*, it would appear that the word began to emerge as something other than a reference to copulation around the middle to late nineteenth century. Similarly, Farmer and Henley's nineteenth-century classic on slang goes beyond the previous exclusive sexual allusion where it defines the word "fucking" as follows:

Adj. (common).—a qualification of extreme contumely.

Adv. (common)—I. Intensive and expletive; a more violent form of BLOODY.

As for its use in public speech, though, we can assume that "fucking" as a nonsexual expletive in English was probably around for a very long time. It was simply not recorded. Sheidlower also took Farmer and Henley's qualification of "common" in the definitions to mean that while they were no doubt employed in common speech, they had been previously unprinted. Since swearing was historically repressed in the printed word, short of using a reliable Ouija board, we will never know what was actually said in public discourse centuries ago. And, with ecclesiastical censorship, as well as natural disasters, such as whole libraries going up in flames and destroying multitudes of hand-written texts, we know precious little of the vernacular. With the increase of the printed word, and a concurrent frankness in literature by the early twentieth century, this or that "fucking something-or-another" was passing from the vernacular into the written word. By the 1920s, the nonfornicative "fucking" could be found in such preeminent authors as Ezra Pound (. . . the fucking lot of 'em), James Joyce (. . . my fucking king), and John Dos Passos (. . . a fucking shame). In addition to "fucking" in this regard, it would be inevitable that writers would soon be emulating the way we spoke by penning a limitless procession of "fucks" in exclamations like, "Fuck you very much!" "What the fuck!" "Fuck it!" or simply, "Fuck!"

Germaine Greer frankly held onto its sexual context as late as 1981 and described it as a lewd term used only by males about "acts performed on the passive female." As questionable as that argument might have been even in 1981, few of us would restrict it to that anymore. Nor would it seem that celebrated authors restrict it at all either. If there ever was someone with all of that time on his hands, it was the individual who scoured through James Kelman's 1994 Booker prize-winning *How Late It Was, How Late*, and tallied that the author had included the word "fuck" over 4,000 times. Being a novel recounting the lives of Scotland's working class, and a not juicy novella about sex acts performed on passive females, that was a heck of a lot of "fucks" for the nonsexual buck—or book. Moreover, considering the widespread and diverse usage of the word today, it is astonishing that a verb that began as a term for a sexual act evolved into an all-embracing generic epithet that is almost patently devoid of sexuality. Is there anything remotely sexual about any of the following phrases? At the same time, is there any single word malleable enough that could be substituted for "fuck"?

"Oh you've gone and fucked it now!" (finite verb)

"Stop fucking around. We've got to get this job done!" (gerund)

"Try not to fuck up this time!" (infinitive)

"Don't fuck with me, mate!" (negative command)

"Get the fuck out of here!" (noun)

"That's fucking ridiculous!" (adverb)

"Fuck! That's a big dog!" (exclamation)

It's the one magical word that—just by its sound—can describe pain, pleasure, hate and love.

To understand the potential that this single word may engender, we need only look at a scene from episode three of the first season of *The Wire*. Two detectives return to a crime scene that had previously turned up no leads. Detective Jimmy McNulty sees something and immediately whispers, "fuck." His fellow detective Bunk Moreland overhears the utterance, and comes over to him. They look at each other in mild if not perplexed revelation. Moreland rejoins with an equally soft but discerning "fuck." For the next five or so minutes, the detectives begin to unravel the clues behind the crime. Tape measures out, and photographs of the murder victim splayed about the floor, the pair purposefully zip around the room studying bullet trajectory angles as they gauge the entry and exit wounds on the victim in the photos until they finally discover a bullet in one of the walls. During the entire search, from initial revelation through puzzlement up until the discovery, the two men only respond to each new development with variously intoned "fucks" or "motherfucks" paralleling their states of mind. Oh, there is a marvelously melodious "fuckity, fuckity, fuckity, fuck, fuck, fuck" upon the unearthing of a particular clue, but no other word is spoken. The word is played with varying intensity as one would otherwise employ background music to heighten a scene without dialogue.

So, how did this shift in a word's initial meaning come about? Sometimes one needs to start in the middle to uncover the muddle, and I think the following bit of graffiti sheds some light on this evolution. Someone scribbled a demeaning epithet about a group of women on a college campus, referring to them as "fucking nymphomaniacs." To this someone scrawled beneath it, "Aren't they all?" First there is the figurative expression that had no intentional link to the sexual root of the word. Connotatively, it was merely used as a derogatory adjective. But it is in the marginalia that we may find a clue to the origin of "fucking" in this context. Taken literally, or denotatively, oaths like "fucking whore" or "fucking bitch" make complete sense; after all, what does a whore do? Still, a literal "fucking whore" has an entirely different context than the figurative "fucking nymphomaniac. Both, however, may have their grounding in the taboo-laden Puritan ethic— positively and negatively. Had the phrase been permissible at the time in literature, Hester Prynne would most assuredly been referred to as a "God-damned whore." It would have been a profound chastisement.

Even if she were referred to as a "God-damned whore, it would not have come from the mouths of women. As Timothy Jay points out, religious women seem to be doubly restricted from cursing," first for their gender (men can express aggression more openly than women can) and second for their religious beliefs (Christians should not use profanity). On the other hand, the growth of "profanity" in the strictest sense of a sacred word used to a secular end was a reaction to the suppressing mores of the deeply entrenched Puritan ethic in America. But bear in mind, as we have seen, that profane means to be secular or indifferent toward religion. Profanity is not an attack on the Church. The latter would be blasphemy. Despite the use of the word "holy" in "holy shit," the phrase is profane as there is no direct attempt to correlate a vulgarism with something spiritual.

Some might argue that "God damn it" is blasphemy and a sin because it flies in the face of the Third Commandment, but such a phrase would probably not cause God to bat an eye because calling upon God to damn something is neither sinful nor unbiblical. In fact, you can find people throughout Scripture, especially in the Psalms, who call upon God to bring judgment on their enemies. In other words, they are asking for God to damn those who they feel are ripe for His judgment. To truly break the Third Commandment, you would need to damage the reputation of God, as in, "God says that if you send in a hundred dollars to my radio program, you will be blessed." Without belaboring the point, there is indeed a fine line between mere profanity and something that will get you in real hot water with the man upstairs. Brad Pitt straddled that line in *Fight Club* (1999) with his menacing pronouncement, "Fuck damnation, man! Fuck redemption! We are all God's unwanted children. So be it!" A major argument of Melissa Mohr's *Holy Shit* is that Judeo-Christian monotheism shifted the center of obscenity from bodily and sexual taboos to oath-making and -breaking. That progression would appear to have come full circle with lines such as the one articulated by the character Debra Morgan on the Showtime series *Dexter*. In the last episode of season seven, aptly titled *Surprise, Motherfucker!*, the supremely potty-mouthed lass who cannot seem to have a conversation without a seemingly mandatory swear word covered both bases with the truly unique, "Well fuck Jesus on a cracker!"

Still, and back to good-old Hester Prynne, just how the so-called Puritan ethic took hold in the early nineteenth century is something of a mystery, because the earlier settlers in America seemed to possess a laxity that diminished with the coming of the next century. If premarital pregnancy is any indication of a looser set of moral strictures, by the 1770s nearly half the women in New England were "with child" at marriage, and approximately 94 percent of Appalachian and other backcountry brides were in a similar state. Bill Bryson also elaborates that "seventeenth- and eighteenth-century users of English, Puritan and non-Puritan alike, had none of the problems with expressive terms like *belly*, *fart*, and to *give titty* (for suckle). . . . But as the eighteenth century gave way to the nineteenth, people suddenly became acutely—and eventually almost hysterically—sensitive about terms related to sex." He puzzles that no one knows why this happened, but while it may have been rooted in Britain, it flowered abundantly in America. "Cockroach" morphed into "roach," titbit" into "tidbit," and "belly" became "tummy." Simple words like "leg," "thigh," and even "stocking" were shunned. These American fears of words would pervade the language for over a century to come. For my own part as a child watching the 1933 film *42nd Street*, I was puzzled by the verbal flub in one of the lines to "Shuffle Off to Buffalo": "He'll do right by little Nelly/ with a shotgun at his . . . be-tummy and away they'll go." The character was obviously about to say "belly," which rhymes with "Nelly," but only much later did I realize that the writer coyly hinted at the word, but did not openly use it because the convention of propriety dictated otherwise. Today it sounds downright silly.

Accordingly, sexually based swearing can be viewed as an act of rebellion, a challenge to an established order, as much as "free love" was in the 1960s. With the former, proponents of open language were rebelling against the idea that words could be dirty, and speaking them freely and without shame was an attempt to remove the taboo that had been placed upon them. Meanwhile, advocates of the latter went directly to the source: to remove the perceived taboo from the act itself. Taking a realistic approach, Allen Walker Read remarked, "The great tragedy of our society is the general failure to achieve warm, outgoing love as the normal relationship between individuals, and the very language itself all too often seems to 'do dirt' on love." The Beatles may have oversimplified the sentiment five years later with their naively optimistic "All You Need Is Love," but their continual repetition of the phrase becomes almost an incantation, or a mantra, that is aimed at setting right that failure. Both Read and the Beatles, I think, would have agreed that somewhere down the line "love" was tainted with a puritanically engendered taboo that subsequently required a rational and positive resolution.

As we have seen throughout history, fear and oppression are often met and repelled by a valiant counterattack: a veritable war on words. Hartogs maintains that one of the functions that obscenity had in American society was "to serve as an outlet for the intolerable tension created within the personality by the opposing cultural polarities of Puritan conformity and the freewheeling search for self." Given the broad sexual repression in the United States, it would only make sense that the sexual revolution would be in the vanguard in the war on words. The 1960s were rife with examples of counterculture defiance in the most literate of circles. There were publications such as Paul Krassner's *Realist* and John Gruen's *The New Bohemian, Avant Garde,* and Broadway was greeted with its share of erstwhile shock-thrills in *O Calcutta!* and *Hair*—the latter, which caused such opprobrium on its release in 1968, was welcomed with nostalgic glee in its 2010 revival. The "fucks" and "shits" in *Hair* were still there, but the effect was no longer scandalous. Hell, everyone now heard those words every day. Disparaging terms were seen in a newer inoffensive light, or "dysphemism," which is the use of a diminutive or offensive word in place of an acceptable one of the same basic meaning (such as calling someone you think is totally cool a "rascal" or "a badass son of a bitch"). As Gershon Legman astutely observed, "The ultimate end of dysphemism is that the obscene or profane word loses all its original meaning, and is used without consciousness of its sexual denotation."

In part this is due to the words or phrases lapsing into cliché or just verbal filler. We all have heard people go into what we may call "you know" jags, when someone robotically suddenly begins cluttering every sentence with "you know." "You know that guy who comes here every day; well, you know what? He's my cousin, you know." Is the speaker truly concerned with the act of knowing in any of the three different ways the phrase was used? Similarly, I doubt if anyone who has ever mouthed the expletive "holy shit" was wittingly alluding to a parcel of sacred excrement. In more genteel days we blurted out strange phrases like "leapin' lizards" and "holy moly." The first of which was hardly meant to induce a mental image of jumping reptiles. As for the latter, it was simple rhyming for emphasis, as in "killer diller," because I doubt if anyone in recent years was aware that moly was a magical herb as well as wild variety of garlic. You know?

As cursing has become less of a taboo, even the original meaning of the word "curse" has mostly gone by the curbside. Initially a curse was a course or series of prayers, especially "prayers of imprecation." It was a "malediction," literally "the speaking of evil. This was in contrast to "benediction"—speaking well of—which in its original meaning denoted a blessing on someone; something we rarely do these days unless someone sneezes. As for cursing, the individual doing it was essentially invoking a higher, supernatural power to send harm to another—call him the cursed.

As an insult, a curse was also meted out as a generic insult. In a curse, you are not picking out any particular shortcoming of your target—say, his stupidity, laziness, or excessive pride. You are instead attacking him in his entirety, declaring him to be unworthy of any of the good things life has to offer. Here is one classic Gypsy curse: "May you wander over the face of the earth forever, never sleep twice in the same bed, never drink water twice from the same well, and never cross the same river twice in a year." Short of stepping in something still warm along the way, it does not get much worse than that. Speaking of "something warm," a popular contemporary affront that has found its way into dozens of films, and was put to music by Margaret Cho and Grant Lee Philips, is "Eat shit and die." It has been overused to the point of banality, but as far as curses go, it does not get much nastier than that.

Turning to the word "curse," its exact origin is somewhat murky, although Eric Partridge thinks that it passed through Old and Middle English from the Latin *coruptus*. What is fairly certain is that by the time it reached Middle English, its specific meaning was to "damn." In this sense, both the *Oxford English Dictionary* and *Webster's Third* point out that the purpose was ecclesiastical: to "excommunicate or anathematize," which roughly means, "May Satan take you," or "Go to the devil." Unless you were a member of the clergy, with a license to curse, cursing or damning someone, as in "May you rot in hell," was a serious calumny. It was taken quite literally, and was often punishable by large fines at the time, because consigning someone to eternal damnation was pretty big stuff. Cursing and damning softened over the years from the infernal implication to basic exasperation or annoyance. Think about when your computer freezes up and shout at the "damned" piece of electronic mayhem. Do you really want it to end up in hell—probably not at least until it reboots and you finish reading your e-mail?

Whereas the religious "word magic" of cursing diminished steadily as the English language shook off the tight constraints of the Church, and the infernal associations all but disappeared, other cultures have still retained the possibility of divine consequences. Islam is but one of many religions where such taboos abound, and Ashley Montagu has pointed out that this could be observed in "the behavior of certain Arabs who, when cursed, ducked their heads or fell flat on the ground in order to avoid a direct hit" of a malediction hurled at them. You might personally duck, too, if someone said, *Kuss Ummak Bisinaan* (Your mother's pussy has teeth). If the sacral import has been driven out of cursing by overuse of the word, unlike the sexual demotion of "fuck," what remains when one curses is the relation to anger that it still intends. Perhaps the most extreme example of this is the song "Fucking Fucking Fuck" by the group Splatpattern. With lyrics like "If you're gonna be a fuck/ Stay the fuck away from me," the song self-aggrandizes itself as "the definitive pissed off anthem of our times." So, when *Network's* "I'm mad as hell, and I'm not going to take it anymore" will not quite cut the mustard, you can sing along with Splatpattern to "vent that spleen."

In another vein, a widespread ambivalence to the purposefulness of religion manifests itself in brutal irony often masked by humor. This should come as no surprise since that combination is at the heart of every successful joke. All humor is fundamentally tragic-comic, because almost anything that can generate laughter can also induce pity if viewed from another perspective. As an example, take the Tony Award–winning, and startlingly popular, musical *The Book of Mormon*, a collaboration between the creators of television's *South Park* (Trey Parker and Matt Stone) and the composer of *Avenue Q* (Robert Lopez). The plot revolves around two pious Mormon missionaries who are sent to do the Lord's work in Africa. As if Mormon's don't have enough trouble with reprobates like myself in the United States, who pretty much slam the door on them when they come a-knocking, these naïfs must confront a one-eyed, genocidal warlord, a group of angry AIDS-infected villagers, and other sacrilegious locals, including one man who claims he has maggots in his scrotum, who are all blaming God for their predicament. Such a theme in a world where Broadway playgoers await yet the next overly produced saccharine Disney blockbuster would seem to spell immediate death on the Great White Way. On the contrary, it opened to raves and was hailed by *New York Times* critic Ben Brantley, who had this to say in his glowing review: "Now you should probably know that is also blasphemous, scurrilous and more foul-mouthed than David Mamet on a blue streak. But trust me when I tell you that its heart is as pure as that of a Rodgers and Hammerstein show." In a culture rooted in religious ideologies, and in a world where much of it is still bound to religious supremacy, swearing "in the name of God"—defiantly or creatively—will not go away any time soon.

And so it is with the recent rise in the proliferation of the nonsexual "fuck" that two entirely different ends have been attained. On one side it may be seen as a liberating force that has broken the yoke of a puritanical heritage by allowing us to freely express ourselves without the shame of sexual recrimination. At the same time it is presenting an endless wellspring for a vast array of casual expletives that in no way reflect the very roots whence they sprang. This liberation should not be taken lightly, for with it came a variety and a versatility of a word that is like no other—in English or any other language. As a means of expression, "fuck" has a continually growing repertoire that is without equal: "dumbfuck," "fuckbrain," "mindfuck," "clusterfuck," or to "Dutch fuck," "Fuck a duck," "monkey or pig fuck," "to fiddle fuck," or "take a flying fuck at the moon." Just the number of uses that are humorous indicates that we have attempted to throw all of our inherited guilt over the four-letter word to the four winds. Repression may have placed a severe onus on the word as a sexual act in the past, but contemporary speakers have mostly reduced the sexual import, and the accompanying taboo.

One of the most au courant, if necessarily neglected medium of study, is the greeting card. That sweeping spawn of Hallmark ranges from the insipid to the salacious, but it is generally timely. It has to be to sell, and even a very good Millard Fillmore joke would never outsell one about George W. Bush. A card I picked up recently depicted a balding, unassuming fellow seated at a window table in a restaurant giving his order to a blasé waiter. The restaurant name, in big, bold red letters above the window was "FUCKER'S." The quote on the outside of the card has the man saying. "I'll have the fuckin' cheeseburger with the fuckin' fries and some fuckin' coffee." Inside, the caption reads, "Happy Fuckin' Birthday."

To turn a phrase, "the fuck doesn't stop here." Its changing use in society represents our changing attitudes toward society itself through the ever-changing language we speak. That's a lot of changes, but language is not only what we say and where we say it, but it is also how we say it: as the greeting card message above illustrates, is it "fucking" or "fuckin'"? Whether you hear a male "nigga" with attitude from the hood enlightening you to the ways of the street, or a prickly female Brit who knows a "fucking asswipe" when she sees one, the enunciations of each are as melodic as they are meaningful. "Woody" or "tinny," meaning carries the day in the end. It is vital to stress this again, but it is the context in which we are using the word that makes all of the difference in the world. For example, "fuck" is immediately perceived as more inflammatory than "screw." After all, the employees at Home Depot would not look at you terribly askance if you asked which aisle had the screws. Depending on how you said it, they even might grin a little to themselves, but they would know what you meant. Taken in different contexts, the phrase "fuckin' A!" as an exclamation of approval generates no rancor, whereas "go screw yourself" most assuredly would.

Similarly, pronunciation, dialect, speech patterns, and nonstandard or ethnic varieties of English all contribute to the influx and output of newer meanings to older words. But as with "fucking whore" or "fucking nymphomaniac," the context, or how those words are distinctly being used, drives it. As Thomas Jay noted, "Tabooness, then, is not universal for all dirty words, but changes with the listener-speaker relationship." "Fucking," as we have seen, is a word that has undergone a complete makeover in the course of the last century due to the freedoms and constraints of social and cultural conditions. A very telling illustration of how "fuck" has been so consummately assimilated into our language may be found—or not found—in the monumental *Dictionary of American Regional English* (DARE). When completed, the five-volume work will have included well over 50,000 entries displaying the patchwork of vernacular Americanisms and colloquialisms, but the specific word "fuck" as an entry appears in a mere four examples: "fuck bug" (love bug), "fuck bump" (an inflamed pimple), "fuck the dog" (to loaf), and "fucky-knuckle" (a play in shooting marbles). That the common variations on the word "fuck" are practically absent from such a copious endeavor reveals how conspicuous the word has risen out of mere colloquialism and has settled comfortably in our everyday speech.

Furthermore, the addition of a commonplace word or two can entirely alter the syntax of a phrase that is totally devoid of any intentional reference to profanity. On a seemingly more innocent note, consider the familiar expression "the mother tongue." Pop in the two little words "of all" and pluralize "tongues," and you will have people wondering exactly what you mean by "the mother of all tongues." Literally or figuratively, words cannot stand alone; they can only be fully understood in relation to the message they are meant to convey. In that respect the context in which language is spoken determines the comprehension and reaction of the listener. Is our choice of graphic expletives just a means of being descriptive, or is it an expression for establishing and possibly rationalizing our personal identities in the real world around us? On a more basic level, have we assimilated the F-bomb into our vocabulary just because it sounds so damned good? In any case, we have come to embrace it not only to signal an emotional release, but also, in the prescient words of Bernard De Voto, "to signify frankness, sophistication, liberalness, companionability, and even smartness"—and while he said this several decades ago, apparently he was not talking to a "fucking wall."

We may also ask who drops the bomb the most, and where? Thanks to the Internet and modern technology, we have something of an answer. According to a piece in *The Atlantic* online, the Ukrainian-based Web development firm Vertaline scanned tweets posted from across 462 specific locations in the United States. The team then isolated particular phrases from those tweets—one of those phrases being, yep, "fuck you," which they tracked between July 14 and July 24, 2012. They then created a dynamic heat map that portrayed the density of the F-bomb-laden tweets as they were distributed geographically throughout each day of their date range, measured once per hour. As one might have suspected, the highest concentrations of F-bombs were correlated with concentrated populations. Unfortunately, the maps are charts of population density rather than per capita rudeness. Still, the maps do indicate that "Big Brother" is not only watching, but also catching fleets of F-bombers out there. Will something replace the word? Although its use is now common, Sheidlower sees no word on the horizon to take its place, largely because other offensive words lack its flexibility.

If we turn our GPS into another direction and travel to Austria, we arrive in a tiny Austrian village in the municipality of Tarsdorf that, despite having a population of only 104, has become famous for its name in the English-speaking world. With a name like Fucking (pronounced *Fooking*), is it any surprise that its road signs are such a popular visitor attraction? The signs were often stolen by souvenir-hunting tourists until 2005, when they were modified to be theft-resistant. Some German beer marketers capitalized on this by naming their light beer—or *helles* beer in German—Fucking Hell (or light beer from Fucking). There were protests, but the Trade Marks and Designs

Registration Office of the European Union agreed with promoter Stefan Fellenberg, who said, "I don't understand why the patents office think of something else. They must have dirty minds." The news came as something to a shock to the mayor of Fucking, Franz Meindl, as the town actually has no brewery.

On a final meandering note, there are some people who believe that "F.U.C.K." is an acronym. One rumor had it that in ancient Britain people could not have sex without royal approval—thus, "Fornication Under Consent of the King." Another has it that the acronym came about in a less-populated England that needed more people to do the necessary daily chores. Here we have "Fornication Under the Command of the King." There are other acronyms, but in the words of *Maledicta*'s erudite editor Reinhold Aman—they're all "100% bullshit." In all likelihood, the word "fuck" did not originate as an acronym. It entered the language fully formed, probably from Dutch or Low German around the fifteenth century. It's impossible to pinpoint, though, probably because it was so taboo that people were afraid to write it down.

3

YOU'RE IN THE FUCKING ARMY NOW!

"Swearing, of course, is not the prerogative of all men.
Many lack the natural gift for it, and others are too timorous."
—H. L. Mencken, *The American Language*

My father-in-law was an elegant man who spoke five languages—six if you count bad language. The latter was seldom spoken in public, but in private among family and friends he could light up the sky with his procession of incandescent oaths. When he caught himself, which was not often, he would then apologize claiming that it was a nasty habit he picked up in the army. Yes, "war is hell," as the saying goes, and a great deal more. My father-in-law was not alone in this predicament. Most of the veterans of the Second World War and the Korean War with whom I have spoken have, like my father-in-law, blamed the military lifestyle and, in particular, life during wartime, as the source for their unbridled profanity. Considering the unfamiliar, trying, and often life-threatening circumstances, who can blame them? It seems to make sense, then, to dive back into in those trenches.

War had been a loosening force for language for several reasons. On a superficial level, once a young fellow put that uniform on, he was a man in a man's world—and mannerisms as well as language followed suit. In part, it was the game of the strutting peacock. Then there was the actual fighting. If a legion of cussing would follow the simple act of chipping an incisor on a ranch-flavored taco chip, think of what losing limbs—yours or anyone else's—would provoke. With so much devastation around, and with the resultant frustration and anger for having to suffer from or render such a degree of violence, how could one not swear? After being accustomed to a relatively comfortable life at home, with wife and family, the soldier was suddenly forced to endure the foulest of living conditions—and strictly in the company of other men. The often-sleep-deprived human body was pressed to the limit. As to be expected, over time, swearing became a matter of course—on and off the battlefield.

Once we have agreed that swearing provides a necessary emotional outlet, it is easy to see that the conscious bottling up of these incendiary feelings could be exceedingly detrimental to the individual soldier as well as those in command. Author Robert Graves pointedly recounts how he was cautioned by peacetime soldiers not to swear at his men. Having had no intention to do so in the first place, this premature rebuke caused him great dismay—until he was on the field of battle: "But after putting the matter to a practical test in trench warfare, I changed my opinion, and later used to advise officer cadets not to restrain their tongues, for swearing had become a universal, but to suit their language carefully to the occasion and to the type of men under their command, and to hold the heavier stuff for intense bombardments and sudden panics."

Accompanying the physical hardships was the psychological strain of war. The onus of death hovered over you. What were mere words next to watching your buddies be ripped to bits and your need to return the slaughter as retribution or just survival? Allen Walker Read, in an article about the F-word—which actually did not include the word itself—commented on the travesties of war and the verbal repercussions: "The soldier, compelled to outrage his inmost nature by killing his fellow human beings, found life topsy-turvy in so many respects that it is small wonder that his observance of taboo was in the inverted manner. . . . With nerves relentlessly exacerbated by gunfire, the unnatural way of life, and the imminence of a hideous death, the soldier could find fitting expression only in terms that according to teaching from his childhood were foul and disgusting." Swearing was a cathartic release—a primal response to the hammer of the gods smashing you to a bloody pulp. If the word "fucking" was used as an adjective to modify every other word of a soldier's speech, "In any light, this would seem appropriate."

The English that Americans speak has been a source of constant derision for many a Brit, from our nation's founding to the present. Some have even claimed that it is incomprehensible. To quote Professor Henry Higgins from *My Fair Lady*, "Why, in America they haven't used it for years." H. L. Mencken observed, "The complaint that Americanisms are inherently unintelligible to civilized Christians is often heard in England, though not as often as in the past." Nevertheless, fighting side by side on the battlefield, Yanks, Brits, and Canadians certainly shared the common vernacular of swearing readily understood by all. American cultural and literary historian Paul Fussell recounts one incident of a group of soldiers entering a church, with one man forgetting to take of his cap. An RAF sergeant-major yanked it off and bellowed, "Take yer fuckin 'at off in the 'ouse of God, cunt!"

In light of this verbal intemperance, there is another curious resonance to swearing that we will come upon from time to time, and that is the power it had when it was omitted. If the pro forma insertion of a four-letter word in a command is suddenly dropped, it is conspicuous in its absence. In the book *Songs and Slangs of the British Soldiers*, editor John Brophy claimed that swearing was so routine that you naturally anticipated your sergeant barking, "Get your — —ing rifles" during the course of a normal day. But if he said,

"Get your rifles!" there was an immediate implication of urgency and danger. Mencken referred to the diminution of the effect of swearing by overuse as dephlogistication. Literally the word means the "removal of phlogiston," which is to say the inherent flammability of an object. His point is well taken in that when a word loses its incendiary power, we must find a substitution, be it another word or the absence of the expected term entirely. The defusing of the F-bomb, and its ensuing replacement by an inoffensive substitute, can be found in the following joke that was popular with American soldiers during World War II. We have seen its passive offspring in an earlier telling, but the original seems to ring with a bit more resolve:

> A soldier is telling about a date he went on with a friend while on leave. "It's the first fucken furlough they gave us in six fucken months, I put my fucken uniform in a fucken locker at the 'Y,' and we went out and had a hell of a fucken time. We picked up two fucken broads in some fucken beer-joint and took 'em to a fucken hotel and laid 'em out on the fucken bed, and had sexual intercourse.

In the later British version we have a "fucking beautiful girl" to whom the teller "makes love." Here we have "two fucken broads" who have "sexual intercourse." The satiric intent may be mutual, but the tone of the original is more a reflection of wartime rather than peacetime.

The extent of swearing must have been so diverse and colorful, if you will, that returning soldiers needed to relearn the genteel language of peacetime. The irony of the veteran's conflicting worlds is illustrated in a joke (within a joke) recounted by Melissa Mohr in *Holy Shit*. A soldier has come back to his family and his grandmother asks him to recount his experiences. Rather than dwell on the horrors of war, he says that the boys sure were funny and had many great jokes. Asked to tell one, he says that he can't because the boys used so much bad language. His grandmother's solution is that the young man insert a blank whenever he comes to a bad word. He agrees and tells one: "Blank blank blank blankity blank. Blank blank blank blank blankity blanking blank blank. Blankity blankity blanking blank, blank blank blank blank fuck."

Women involved in the war effort were no strangers to the changing attitudes toward swearing. Even those women who stayed home to work in the service of the military arms industry evidently also fell under the spell of public swearing as evidenced from a Philadelphia aircraft factory in this waggish twist on the cautioning phrase "Ladies present": NO SWEARING. THERE MAY BE GENTLEMEN PRESENT. Taken at face value, the sign evokes a chuckle—ah, but underneath! The war years saw a marked shift in traditional attitudes to gender roles in society as well. Wonder Woman first appeared in comics, and Rosie the Riveter became an icon for the female blue-color worker in wartime. The Broadway stage also became a venue for the growing support for feminist awareness, which is particularly evident in the wartime hit *Bloomer Girl*. For starters, the heroine, played by Celeste Holme, is appropriately named Evelina Applegate. She joins her aunt Dolly Bloomer in a crusade for the abolition of slavery and for the cause of women's rights, and the show-stopping song "It Was Good Enough for Grandma," with lyrics by Yip Harburg, is a feisty anthem to women's liberation.

In it he writes that Grandma was a lady, who sewed and cleaned and cooked, and did all the household chores. Meanwhile, grandfather was the boss. Applegate then sings that it may have been good enough for grandma, "it ain't good enough for us."

One may wonder what sort of response that fervid, if not downright ballsy sentiment elicited from the audience upon hearing a female utter line, "And that's a *hell* of a fate!" It was a gutsy play filled with bravado. But when the show closed in 1946, the war was at an end, and the home front was returning to its prewar conventions—not to ignore the fact that men wanted their jobs back. The same government agencies that had encouraged women to give up their roles as happy housewives and take on the work that men left behind were now asking them to resume their previous lives as homemakers. It was only natural that, like the men who returned from the war with their crusty vocabulary, the women of that Philadelphia aircraft factory also needed to learn to curb their cursing. The swearing remained, but it had respectfully gone underground.

As much as one could wish it so, swearing does not have a switch that you can turn off simply because you're in your barracks safe and sound or back home in the privacy of your den to make it so. Moreover, as a veteran of the Second World War told me, it was "in-fucking-possible" to return to his prewar manner of speech, just as it was practically impossible to resume a pacific daily routine of going to work and coming home after having participated in a war that eradicated a good portion of the human race. Still, these veterans did gradually manage to curtail their wartime swearing when they returned because of the stigma of shame very much attached to cursing in public. It was not an easy chore, particularly since it felt so good to freely vocalize your feelings.

For those men who remained in the armed forces, colorful cursing and swearing from NCOs up to the brass was de rigueur. Whether near to the front line or far from the immediate dangers of combat, there was no shortage of swearing among troops. It served to instill bonding. Like recovering alcoholics, even those soldiers who never had to face combat needed some self-imposed camaraderie to reconcile their newer unfamiliar, dictatorial, and often claustrophobic surroundings, and they, too, were just as inundated with the jargon. Why not revel in this new-found freedom to blurt out what you had been forbidden to say as a young child or as a circumspect adult? All at once the soldier was a child frightened by the perilous unknown, as well as the teen who was challenging authority, and finally as the wizened adult who realized that no matter what, he was not the master of his own fate—he was "fucked."

Of course, this is not to say that swearing in wartime was not without its sense of humor. Indeed, what remotely sane person would deny that a little humor goes a long way to relieve the stress of formidable situations? The army naturally could not embrace war as a favorable activity, so it fostered an ambivalent love-hate relationship with all things military. From life-threatening situations right down to the forgettable edibles designated as army chow, the soldier was expected to display a requisite aversion. Some G.I.s may not have eaten better in their lives, but their chipped beef on toast was still "shit on a shingle." My father often spoke fondly about "SOS." (But that may have been less out of nostalgia; when it came to cooking, my mother was something of an assassin in the kitchen).

This feisty contrariety carried over into daily routine. It seemed to demand that you be contrary and that you object to everything. This was the army, and you were taught to fight. This included fighting the army that ordered you about. If euphemism was a passive suppression of negative expressions in exchange for positive ones, dysphemism was an unmitigated flaunting of actively negative substitutions. Dysphemism was everywhere, and almost everything resounded with cantankerous swearing—even the best situations. The French writer Albert Carnoy succinctly summed up the difference: "Dysphemism is a stimulant, whereas euphemism is a sedative." The soldier awaiting his pay eagerly looked forward to "the eagle shitting on Friday." Of course, things were not always rosy during wartime, and this afforded the soldier to do his worst, or best, in this department. Think of that ubiquitous acronym we still use when matters go awry: SNAFU—Situation Normal: All Fucked Up. There were many other army terms as well that have not had the longevity of SNAFU, like FUMTU (Fucked Up More Than Usual), while FUBAR (Fucked Up Beyond All Recognition) seems to be making the rounds again with the college drinking set, for "extremely drunk." With acronyms abounding, not all were derisive, even if many had a touch bawdiness: NORWICH ([K]Nickers Off Ready When I Come Home). Nobody seemed to be immune to imaginative petulance or creative prurience, and it may come as a surprise to some to learn that Theodore Geisel, the man who would one day be known as Dr. Seuss, penned many humorous cartoons for the soldiers featuring anatomical parts, racial slurs, and, of course, swearing a red, white, and blue streak.

With the pervasion of swearing, curbing one's tongue could result in a hilarious response, simply because you might have been at a loss for the sanitized words. Robert Graves recounts an incident when a soldier, who was shot in the buttocks, was asked by a visiting duchess inquiring where he was wounded. "I wouldn't know," the man replied. "I never learned no Latin." If the reality of swearing in uniform was universal, the public portrayal of the military man on the screen and in literature was severely mollified. General George Patton was both famous and infamous for his swearing. The speech he made to his soldiers before they went into battle on D-Day was riddled with his unique style of profanity: "Let the first bastards to find out be the Goddamned Germans. Someday I want to see them raise up on their piss-soaked hind legs and howl, 'Jesus Christ, it's the Goddamned Third Army again and that son-of-a-fucking-bitch Patton.'" The George C. Scott film of 1970 retained some of the "shit" and "God-damns" in the speech that opened Patton, but the oration was clearly sanitized for public viewing.

With the realism portrayed in cinema of the late twentieth century about wars, it would be downright ludicrous to hear Sergeant Bulldog Ballbuster limit his cussing to "Oh sugar, boys." And Norman Mailer's aberrant "fug" would surely give rise to curious stares once reserved for the likes of albino hippos and two-headed rattlesnakes. It was only three years after Mailer's Naked and the Dead was published, in 1951, when James Jones created a stir for his use of "fuck" in the best-selling *From Here to Eternity*. Today it is impossible to imagine a contemporary realistic account, whether it be a book or a film, that would omit it. For some people, though, realism has its place, and it's not necessarily in reality—or on the television screen. The 1998 Oscar-winning Steven Spielberg World War II film *Saving Private Ryan* had already aired on network television in 2001, but when it was scheduled to be shown on Veterans Day of 2005, at least 65 of 225 ABC stations said they wouldn't air it for fear of being fined by the FCC. How could this change come about? Well, stations were especially wary because of recent heavy fines imposed upon CBS for airing its Janet Jackson "wardrobe malfunction" during a Super Bowl halftime, and they were afraid of getting slapped with the same. The *Chicago Tribune* responded with, "Unlike Ms. Jackson's breast, the saucy language in Spielberg's film has redeeming social value, to use the U.S. Supreme Court's famous phrase. Its language, like its brutal violence, is an integral part of the riveting realism that makes the Oscar-winning movie a uniquely effective cinematic tribute to the heroism of ordinary Americans at war."

On the other side of the debate, the American Family Association praised those stations banning it claiming that "*Ryan's* language— which included at least 20 'F' words and 12 'S' words—is not suitable for children watching at 8 p.m. It may be OK on the battlefield, but it's not OK on the public airwaves during prime-time broadcast hours." While they may have believed that the preemptive move reflected TV's increasing concerns about indecency questions, it was obviously more likely that those stations were covering their commercially financed hinders. With regard to fines, the ABC parent station said it would cover any that were issued, but there were none. Those ABC affiliates that did show the film, which was introduced by Vietnam veteran Senator John McCain, gave their audiences a gritty, realistic look at war. Apparently a number of ABC affiliates that did not air *Ryan* treated their viewers with another thrilling blockbuster: *Return to Mayberry*.

Following their choice not to air the film, many of those stations were bombarded with countless phone calls, clearly indicating the general public was not averse to hearing the purported foul language in a crucial historical context. Then, of course, they were by far more accustomed to hearing it publicly than the general public of generation ago—which takes us to the language used by the present-day military. Chances are that soldiers of recent devastations, such as the war in Afghanistan and the two Iraq wars, have gone off to battle already loaded with an arsenal of swear words and expressions they had learned in everyday life back at home. Bad language was nothing new to the men and women who stormed off to the First Iraq War. This predilection for swearing presents a fundamental difference between the returning soldiers from earlier wars, and those returning from more recent conflagrations. War may have been "hell" in the 1940s, but by the 1990s that simply would not do. The thunder of distant guns, the cascading rain of rocket fire, and city blocks going up in flames and raging long into the night had become "hellacious." True, the little-known word had been around since the early 1930s in slang as anything remarkably bad or good, but it was dredged up from obscurity during Operation Desert Storm by reporters who needed something more fearsome than the nearly deadened "hell." War wasn't just hell anymore, war was hellacious.

Once again the media did its part to report the frenzied course of events, and the latest technologies available to them allowed them to do so with remarkable accuracy and expected sensationalism. In another vein, the new technologies more easily afforded videographers the means to reveal the truth behind the successes and mistakes of the United States in its war efforts, especially beginning with the War in Afghanistan and the 2003 Iraq War. With the spontaneity of emotional swearing, reporters spit out their gut reactions to what they saw, and it was instantly transmitted to millions. Intrepid filmmakers Tim Hetherington and Sebastian Junger created a scalding documentary titled *Restrepo* about the brutality of the War in Afghanistan. In keeping with the propriety imposed upon us when sat down before a camera, the soldiers interviewed off the battlefield were guarded in their swearing. Off camera, with random gunfire assaulting them from the distant mountaintops and ravines of the Korangal Valley, though, the swearing became vastly more prodigious. Although it has not aired on network television, one wonders if the American Family Association would praise TV stations for not presenting this brutal side of war. The A.F.A will have no chance to take further issue with Hetherington's vérité, however, as the filmmaker was killed during his work on a new documentary about the insurgents battling Colonel Muammar el-Qaddafi in Libya.

The previous veterans, like my father-in-law, may have attempted to "unlearn" the vocabulary they tossed about so freely, while our present-day veterans are just going back to the same world of swearing that they had departed in the first place—wiser to the ways and wiles of the world, perhaps, but not necessarily apologetic regarding their description of it.

Just to turn briefly to the shock value of swearing—or lack thereof—involving a brutal event off the battlefield, a trip to Fenway Park might not have only offered you the highest priced beer in baseball, but it also showed how civilians react when faced with the anger over their own tragedy. While Boston essentially shut down on the Friday after the deadly bombing at the 2013 marathon, and police combed the region for the second assailant, the Red Sox canceled their scheduled game. The next day, however, with the alleged bomber in custody, the town flaunted its resilience. The Red Sox game against the Kansas City Royals was preceded by an emotional pregame ceremony that honored the victims of the horrific attacks. On the playing field, Red Sox star David "Big Papi" Ortiz, microphone in hand, had this to say to the Boston fans: "This jersey that we're wearing today, it doesn't say 'Red Sox.' It says, 'Boston.' We want to thank you, Mayor Menino, Governor

Patrick, the whole police department, for the great job that they did this past week." Then, with his fist in the air and defiance in his voice, he added, "This is our fucking city. And nobody is going to dictate our freedom. Stay strong." The stadium shook with thunderous applause. In any other situation, where a player swore in front of thousands of fans and during a televised game, he would have been fined. Perhaps knowing the subsequent rancor of Sox fans, the FCC gave Ortiz a free pass; nor was there a reason to explain his remark to the little kids munching $4.50 wieners what it was he said. I've been to Fenway, and I know.

4

SWEARING, A GAME ANYONE CAN PLAY

*"I can't think of anything, any mission, more important
for a political party or for our candidate than the mission
of restoring honor and dignity to the Oval Office."*
—Dick Cheney, at a Philadelphia campaign rally
August 4, 2000

"Does anyone ever say 'fuck you'? I don't care if they do."
—George W. Bush, in *Talk Magazine*
(1999 interview with Tucker Carlson)

Given our routine exposure to four-letter words, it may come as a
surprise to learn that it was not until 1959 that the ban on D. H.
Lawrence's *Lady Chatterley's Lover*, an already recognized literary
classic, was finally in the United States. It was in July of that year that
the ban—along with the ban on *Tropic of Cancer* and *Fanny Hill*—
was overturned in court with assistance by publisher Barney Rosset
and lawyer Charles Rembar. It was then published by Rosset for Grove
Press, finally allowing people to purchase the complete novel that
had previously only been available in an abridged version in America.

(Its translation was still banned in Japan until the 1970s—if you can believe that!) In 1928, soon after its publication, it had enough people swooning that even the Senate decided to act. Then Utah Senator Reed Moot declared, "It was so disgusting, so dirty and vile that the reading of one page was enough for me. I've not taken ten minutes on *Lady Chatterley's Lover*, outside of looking at its opening pages. It is most damnable! It is written by a man with a diseased mind and a soul so black that he would obscure even the darkness of hell!" I think we would all agree that this is a "moot" point indeed.

Moot or not, the decency-minded senator had comrades in armed enforcement, most notably Anthony Comstock. As government appointed special agent for the U.S. Post Office, he and his men enforced the Comstock Act by seizing millions of books, photographs, contraceptives, and anything they remotely judged as obscene. Braving rain, snow, heat, and gloom of night, he proudly saw to it that his efforts had led to the imprisonment of 36,000 people and caused fifteen suicides. Over the course of the century the act gradually lost its impact, but, ironically, it is still technically on the books today—so, you better watch out when bringing in anything in plain brown wrappers. In a further irony, it came out that Comstock was barely literate, but even if he knew nothing about art, he knew what he did not like.

An oft-quoted prudish remark was, "I never heard such language!" To this, one wag replied, "Then how do you know what it means?" In an earlier instance, shortly after Dr. Samuel Johnson published his famous dictionary, a literary lady complimented him upon it and particularly expressed her satisfaction that he had not admitted any improper words. "No, Madam," he replied, "I hope I have not daubed my fingers. I find, however, that you have in looking for them." Still, *Lady Chatterley* was an example of the written word that was meant to be read, not heard, so the prude did have a point there, because one simply did not say those words aloud in mixed company. By 1959, though, most everyone was unquestionably familiar with those very words that had led books by Lawrence, James Joyce, Henry Miller, and even Robert Burns to be confiscated by customs agents on the Hudson River Piers. Apart from seemingly allowing for greater freedom in the arts, vindication of *Lady Chatterley* should have had little effect on the language of a public so well acquainted with the words therein.

Or maybe not, as Renatus Hartogs, a Dutch-born New York psychiatrist, elaborated on this in his incisive *Four-Letter Word Games*. Attending a party in Bellport, Long Island, the Saturday following the decision, Hartogs was quite amazed at how the reverse ruling dominated the conversation—in theoretical and in actual discussion. Accordingly, four-letter words had suddenly become legitimate news, and as debates ensued he recalls with amusement at "hearing a string of barracks words paraded with a crisp Vassar inflection. In fact, it was mostly the women who kept the talk going. The men, for the most part, seemed subdued." His reasoning was that many of the men must have felt uncomfortable because they had, in other circumstances and other company, used the very same words. To now hear the word "fuck" bandied about was a challenge to an established order. Hartogs went on to say that Lawrence could hardly have expanded anyone's vocabulary, but the erstwhile complex of taboos that had kept those words in public check were, like the book itself, liberated.

The following anecdote has been attributed to several regarding the very prim Loretta Young and one of the guests to her show, but I trust Stephen Sondheim's recollection: Ethel Merman was known for swearing during rehearsals and meetings. While rehearsing a guest appearance on NBC's *The Loretta Young Show*, she was told that since Young could not abide foul language she would have to pay $1 each time she swore. As she was being shoehorned into an ill-fitting gown for the next number Merman exclaimed, "Oh shit, this damn thing's too tight." Young advanced on her waving her curse box and said, "Come on Ethel, put a dollar in the box. You know my rules." Merman's retort reportedly was, "Ah, honey, how much will it cost me to tell you to go fuck yourself?"

Of course, swear words are not easily pigeon-holed. A calculated insertion of "fuck" at the right moment and with proper elocution could serve any number of masters. As Hartogs maintains, "With a judiciously dropped four-letter bon mot we can, in sophisticated circles, be at the same time rebellious and respectable, prim and prurient."

And the timing could not have been better. The '60s and '70s also marked the emergence of greater personal freedoms that manifested themselves in attitudes of liberation from the accepted norms in attitudes, dress, and free speech. The growing explicit language in literature was justified by its defenders as the way people actually talked. Detractors argued that a proliferation of such language promoted greater use of it in public, and that swearing in an art form seemingly served to legitimize it. This vindication, one might argue, would thereby further the use of four-letter words among people who would otherwise have been more circumspect in this regard. Add to this an expanding media, and the use of words as symbols of freedom, forms of shock, or examples of cleverness has created an open forum for anyone with a voice and a motive. Take for example the use of "fuck" by 2004 presidential candidate John Kerry in the *Village Voice* or former Vice President Dick Cheney's direct "Fuck you" to Vermont Senator Patrick Leahy on the Senate floor—and to much applause of his fellow Republicans at that. In subsequent interviews, Cheney waffled from admitting that he used harsh language, and felt good afterward, to denying that he said it at all. Public reaction was less of chastisement than it was of respect for two men who had the balls enough to choose "directness over convention." Perhaps, but in the film *Curtain Call*, Michael Caine's character oppugns James Spader's usage of it as "the riposte of the inarticulate."

Similarly, when Donald Trump lets loose a salvo of "fucks" and "motherfuckers" at his detractors during his talks, the audience cheers at his forthright audacity. At least it keeps them from remarking on the double comb-over. So, whether it is the physical act of whacking your thumb with a hammer with that ball-peen, or fending off sudden verbal attacks with the F-bomb, spontaneity, whether precognitive or cognitive, is still the motivation here. In a noteworthy aside, the United States Senate passed a Broadcast Decency Enforcement Act on the same day as Cheney's verbal assault. The vote was ninety-nine to one—another win for the hypocritically correct.

Presidents as well are not immune from swearing. After the 2010 BP oil spill, President Barack Obama, while speaking to Matt Lauer on the *Today* show, vowed that he was talking to experts "so I would know whose ass to kick." According to presidential historian Robert Dallek, "The public finds it appealing that he's being strong-willed and speaking his mind. But presidents need to be restrained and operate in rational, thoughtful ways as well. They can't go half-cocked, explosive, emotional. That's not very appealing to the public." At least it was not the F-bomb. But we can turn to other presidents, or vice presidents, for that. It made the news that when President Obama was preparing to sign his health-care bill Vice President Joe Biden whispered in the president's ear that the legislation he was about to sign was a "big fucking deal." If Obama's "ass" and Biden's "BFD" are great fodder for the news media, the initial public reaction is usually less critical. Biden's gaffe was so amusing to some that "BFD" T-shirts were sold at the time. Subsequently, the "BFD" was resurrected for a new round of T-shirts when Obamacare was upheld by the Supreme Court in June 2012.

President Richard Nixon, courtesy of the presidential tapes, is probably the most notable head of state known for swearing, and it is because of him that we now have the ubiquitous term "expletive deleted." Indeed, there were some fifty-nine expletives deleted from the tapes, and the term gained such notoriety that protesters demanding Nixon's resignation flaunted banners reading IMPEACH THE

[EXPLETIVE DELETED]! Of course, not everything Nixon said was safely corralled. But while the rants, "Fuck you, motherfucker. . . . It's not funny after a while" or "Fuck [Chief-Justice Berger]. Let him resign. Fuck the ABA [American Bar Association]!" did slip through the gates, one must keep in mind that these remarks were intended to be strictly off the record. Moreover, Nixon was usually extremely cautious about using the word in public. In one instance, his restraint by today's standards might even seem laughable. Perhaps he was just trying to be one of the guys on a break during the Frost-Nixon interviews when he asked Frost, "David, did you do any fornicating this weekend?"

Or is it laughable? Next to George W. Bush's "Fuck Saddam. We're going to take him out!" or "You fucking son of a bitch. I saw what you wrote. We're not going to forget this" (in 1986 to then *Wall Street Journal Washington*'s Al Hunt in a Dallas restaurant in front of other diners, Hunt's wife, and his four-year-old son), Nixon's use of the perfectly acceptable word "fornicating" comes across as downright crude, if not creepy. Similarly, Rahm Emanuel, renowned for his loose lips, chastised liberals who vowed to go after moderate and conservative Democrats not yet aboard on the same health-care reform bill mentioned above as "Fucking retarded!" He was forced to apologize, though not to the liberal Democrats, or for his dropping the F-bomb. He was admonished for using the word "retarded," which was itself a euphemism at one time. The conservative right is not without its own irony. The traveling press secretary for Mitt Romney, Rick Gorka, lost his cool and cursed at reporters who attempted to ask questions of the Republican presidential candidate near the Tomb of the Unknown Soldier in Warsaw. Just what was he thinking when he said, "Kiss my ass. This is a holy site for the Polish people. Show some respect." One would only imagine that it was not a particularly holy site for Mr. Gorka.

Nixon may unfairly be remembered as our foulest-mouth president, but that is through what we surmise rather than what we actually know. For that matter, he probably swore no more than John Kennedy or Lyndon Johnson. In interviews with Gore Vidal, Kennedy was quoted as saying, "In this job, the worse you fuck up, the higher the ratings" and, "If they want this job, fuck 'em. They can have it!" But it was Johnson who did it with such flair. Leave it to the great southern gentleman to give us, "Ford's economics are the worst thing to happen to this country since pantyhose ruined finger-fucking." To be equitable, presidential swearing has an even longer and more venerable pedigree. One can point to the salty language supposedly mouthed by Lincoln in Steven Spielberg's film of the same name. Audiences may have been taken aback, and possibly even disbelieving, by the president's off-color jokes, and yet, for many years after his assassination, the "Illinois Rail-Splitter" was remembered not only for his fortitude but also for his liberal usage of cuss words. Mencken had this to say about him: "Lincoln, had there been no Civil War, might have survived in history chiefly as the father of the American smutty story." This quote comes from a book whose title in itself was quite shocking for 1918, *Damn! A Book of Calumny*. (I may be wrong, but I doubt if anyone reading this book of the same title is particularly nonplussed.) Mencken himself was somewhat uncomfortable with the title, as he explains in his introduction. This, however, did not prevent the book from going through four editions in the very first year of publication. To conclude the quote just mentioned, Mencken sardonically had this to say about the "American smutty story—the only original art-form America has yet contributed to literature." Fifty shades of blue?

Unfortunately, anyone in the public spotlight is under the most excessive scrutiny. This is particularly so of celebrities who are almost expected to expose themselves in public. While accepting the Best Supporting Actor trophy from Kirk Douglas at the 2011 Oscars, Melissa Leo offhandedly said, "Kate did it two years back, and she made it look so fucking easy!" Realizing what she had done on global television, she then added, "Oops! I am so sorry!" Judging from the big round of applause and laughter from the audience, it appeared that she neither shocked anybody nor intended to. The use of the F-word in this context had no sexual, immoral, or obscene implications. One might even venture to say, "No harm done." Even so, Leo apologized again the next day, probably at the urging of someone else, because her comment was more of a rationalization than an apology: "I had no idea. This word. . . . I apologize to anyone that they offended." Bear in mind that this is an actress who just won an Academy Award based upon a character who was using the very same language on screen. Ironically, the very award presented to an actor because of her ability to emote and explode with four-letter words on the screen was slapped on the wrist for delivering but a wee bit of that film character in public. Had she said "oh, sugar" or "fiddle-dee-dee" throughout the film, that Oscar would now be perched on someone else's mantelpiece.

One of the most famous cases of swearing on television came after a January 2003 NBC broadcast of the Golden Globe Awards, in which U2 lead singer Bono uttered the phrase "fucking brilliant." The FCC said the F-word in any context "inherently has a sexual connotation" and can lead to enforcement. The networks challenged the policy, and an appeals court found that the FCC had violated federal law covering how agencies make regulations. The Supreme Court reversed that decision, saying the FCC gave a sufficient explanation to comply with the law and asked the appeals court to reevaluate the indecency rules. The appeals panel, however, agreed with the networks that the FCC had failed to let them know which words are "patently offensive" for purposes of its policy. As an example, they cited that whereas the FCC concluded that "bullshit" in an *NYPD Blue* episode was patently offensive, the very same FCC concluded that "dick and dickhead" were not. Eventually the FCC conceded the Bono case, saying that "fucking" was indeed used as a demonstrative adjective and not as an invitation to intercourse. Wise as the FCC may have been in its reversal, it still needed to learn that Bono's use of the word was as an adverb and not as an adjective.

Let us slip back into our eveningwear and return to the 2011 Oscars. Over the course of the evening, other actors jokingly alluded to the remark, getting yet another laugh with each reference to it. Anyone watching the Oscars on television did not hear the actual dropping of the F-bomb, though, courtesy of ABC's "bleeping" it via their seven-second delay, but it was not likely that most viewers did not know what she had said. If the Hollywood audience applauded loudly at hearing it firsthand, and home viewers readily inferred what was bleeped out, how effective is such censorship? In the context of changing cultural values, what once was a weighty shield keeping taboos under cover is becoming a transparent veneer. If we can all see through it, what good is it? Melissa Leo's expletive was an Oscar first—and a first usually means that there will be more to come. It is quite telling that in her ostensible apology she added, "There's a great deal of the English language that is in my vernacular. I really don't mean to offend, and it's probably a very inappropriate place to use that particular word." When she said "probably," it implied that she herself was uncertain about swearing in public—at least in the circles with which she is familiar. If anything, the benevolent reaction to her "fucking easy" easily demonstrates that those circles are rapidly expanding.

Another observation may be made regarding the incident, and that is the none-too-secret fact that women are swearing in a way that was previously assumed to be the sole province of men. Timothy Jay, and especially Tony McEnery, have cited examples in the 1990s and list charts detailing the frequency with which men swear more abusively than women. And, in his stimulating *Blue Streak*, Richard Dooling devoted an entire chapter to "Why Men Swear More Than Women": "Because men are congenitally incapable of indulging in good, long cries, swearing provides them with a handy compromise when presented with the impractical alternatives of running away, crying, or fighting. Men can be hostile creatures, and swearing often allows them to exchange oaths instead of blows."

Dooling penned his words in 1996, but I think that even as he wrote them, the role of women in society had changed radically. Clearly, some reading today might also take exception with his quote's essentialist sexism. Women were taking their proper place in the workforce and commanding jobs of authority and responsibility once relegated to men, much as they had done during the war, but this time they were staying. Consequently, the language barrier that the more prudish among us believed to exist between men and women was shattered for good. Just ask Tina Fey. During the 2013 Golden Globe Awards, she and *Saturday Night Live* compatriot Amy Poehler tossed some light-hearted catty quips at the country music cutie, Taylor Swift. This caused the latter to say, or perhaps hiss, to *Vanity Fair*, "There's a special place in hell for women who don't help other women." Naturally the paparazzi jumped all over this, hounding Fey, no doubt trying to stir the hornet's nest even more. *E! News* has video footage that shows fed-up Fey totally brushing off one photographer who asked if she thought Swift overreacted to the joke. Fey responded by laughing and telling him, "Go fuck yourself." Forget what I said earlier: it may be prudent not to ask Tina Fey. This is not to say that all men and women will swear and speak freely with each other without reservations, but they do not mutually engage in conversations about jock itch or cellulite either. After all, even in an ideal world where a much-hoped-for equality thrived, I would like to think that there still would be a couple of appreciable differences remaining between the sexes.

5

"ALL THE NEWS THAT'S FIT TO PRINT"

"There's a dirty paper, using sex to make a sale,
The Supreme Court was so upset, they sent him off to jail."
—Phil Ochs, "A Small Circle of Friends"

Writing in *Made in America*, Bill Bryson pondered, "Never before or since has there been a more confused and bewildering age. To read on the one hand that the *New York Times* castigated women for saying *What a cunning hat*, and, on the other, Angela Heywood publicly arguing for the right to say *fuck* makes it all but impossible to believe that we are dealing with the same people in the same country in the same century." Yes, the country was the United States, but the century was the end of the nineteenth. The first reference is to a *Times'* editorial sternly admonishing women against the growing use of slang in that it betokened a dangerous laxity of morals. The above sentence, "What a cunning hat," was an example of that dangerous moral laxity. The latter reference is to the early feminist Angela Heywood who objected to being required to use the phrase "generative sexual intercourse" in her lectures. As she put it, "Three words, twenty-seven letters to define a given action . . . commonly spoken in one word of four letters that everybody knows the meaning of." The *Times* may not use generative sexual intercourse in its stead, as it is more likely to use the phrase "four-letter word," because, at least as of this writing, the paper is one of the last bastions in journalism to disdain the use of the word "fuck."

But the *Times* is not alone in its loathing "to contribute to a softening of the society's barriers against harsh or profane language." When Sam Zell, the owner of the Tribune newspapers, cursed at an *Orlando Sentinel* staff photographer in 2008, the *Los Angeles Times* (another Tribune paper) wrote that Zell threw a "two-word obscenity" at her. *Los Angeles Times* contributing editor Gustavo Arellano said that the paper should reflect the ownership. He wrote the following in a column:

> *"Now, I understand that* The Times *still considers itself a family newspaper, one in which bad words don't exist and sex ads get exiled to the classifieds section. . . . And I agree that the gratuitous use of profanity can cheapen an august institution. . . . But it's one thing to publish an unedited Howard Stern rant or print a transcript of the latest Paris Hilton sexcapades; it's quite another when the vulgarity itself is the story. And in the case of Zell, and other public figures who stir up a fuss for the words they use,* The Times *fails spectacularly.*

In response to the recent concern over profanity in public journalism, the Temple University law Web site Journalism in Society posed the following question to its readers: Should newspapers and broadcast news outlets start running curse words as people use them? Or do we have a deeper responsibility to the public?

One reader responded, "It would totally offensive [sic] if newspapers start publishing curse words. That would be very unprofessional and tacky, especially towards our elders who read newspapers and watch the news." That reader was in the small minority of 14 percent of the respondents. Most of the readers agreed with Arellano in that omitting them may put a nebulous slant on the story. One of the more representative responses asserted: "Kudos to Arellano. His article isn't calling for writers to use so-called obscene words in their stories as part of their own, personal language, but rather when an important quote contains the word. It is an entirely different issue than I think most people are making it out to be here, and he's right. After all, we can't be completely objective if forced to explain someone else's words, yeah?"

One argument that is continually brought up, and primarily dealt with in another chapter later, is that language should be guarded to protect the children. Rubina Ali of the Department of Journalism at the University of Illinois succinctly rebukes this notion: "We seem to think people will be extremely offended if we include profanity in our writing, but when quoting a heavy-hitter in a story, it just makes the story more colorful. People have this notion that children may see it and be negatively affected but the truth is, 1. Children usually don't read the newspaper as it is and 2. A lot of the most commonly used swear words can be heard on the playground already." While the comment about children seems to be at the heart of Ali's assessment, she glosses over an equally, if not more pressing, issue—that of "heavy hitters." As Claire O'Conner (no relation to James of Cuss Control) remarks, "But surely when the word in question is part of a direct quote from a person in power, it should be included in full—not only in the interest of accuracy, but also in the interest of treating readers like savvy, 21st century adults, rather than prim Victorians reaching for the smelling salts at the sight of a four-letter word."

This takes us back to the incident of Vice President Biden dropping the F-bomb within public earshot. First, however, it is significant to note that O'Conner's article appeared in the *Columbia Journalism Review*, a major journal that until only recently opted for the substitution of "the F-word" as a modest alternative to "fuck." Addressing both matters of protecting children and proper reportage, *Guardian*'s David Marsh asserted, "But I do feel strongly that we have a duty to treat our readers as adults, not children, and quote people accurately, not decide which words our readers can or cannot handle. The Biden story is a case in point. Everyone knows he said 'big fucking deal', so the media have achieved nothing by not reporting his words accurately apart from making themselves look out of touch with the real world."

In fairness to the *Times*, which chose not to include Biden's direct quote, and opted instead to coyly—but objectively—print "Mr. President, this is a big . . . deal," adding later that the adjective between the big and the deal begins with "f," other papers subjectively focused on their estimations of the gravity of the word itself. An editorial in the more conservative *Hartford Courant* disparagingly referred to the incident as "Biden's F-Bomb: A Blunder That Sullied a Historic Moment." The *Courant* was not alone in their shame-game, which clearly separates American journalism from its British counterpart. Across the shining sea, the *Guardian*, *Observer*, and *Independent* all quoted Biden in full after comment. As Richard Adams, the *Guardian* reporter who covered Biden's gaffe, explained it: "If Joe Biden says something is a 'big fucking deal,' that is germane to the story."

Referencing *Lady Chatterley's Lover*, journalist Melvin J. Lasky observed, "Lawrence's venture into sexual discourse had been justified on grounds of its 'literary merit.' The prose of daily journalism was far removed from those heights." Although wary of the quality of journalism in general, the point Lasky went on to make was that while there are papers like the *Evening Standard* devoted to the principles of high culture and proper language, they could still be skittish about reporting the accuracy of events. He highlights this by citing an article using the phrase "in a bizarre joke . . . [Slattery] used a four-letter word to describe de Jongh . . . ." To this Lasky puzzled, "Well, what *had* he said?" The *Standard* may have been recounting an incident that was meant to incite outrage in the reader over a salacious comment a foul-mouthed comedian had made to one of its own most respected columnists, but not having been given the scandalous details, "a curious reader was plunged into darkness." Whatever the word was, it was truly germane to the story, and rather than present a seemingly newsworthy event with an eye on fact and precision, the article floundered in speculation.

There is one other aspect about the written word that should also be considered: its sound. Stub your little toe on the foot of the bed, spill your beer on your lap, forget your keys in your car, and you suddenly find yourself muttering a miscellany of formidable expletives. With the subsiding of pain, the dried off pants, and the hundred dollars spent to have someone jimmy your car door, those cusswords will have been forgotten—although the latter resolution may well inspire a fresh batch of expletives. But pick up a book or a newspaper and read any one of those four-letter words you just randomly uttered and "listen" to it jump off the page. It is rather like listening to our voice as we speak compared to listening to someone else's, or even our own via a recording. In the first instance, our brains emit the sound, whereas in the second, our brains step back and process it. Similarly, if we happen upon just one of Carlin's seven words in print, each seems to resonate with greater punch than if we offhandedly speak them. This may be because we are engaging three sensory organs instead of two to process it. All in an instant we see the word first, and then we speak it to ourselves, and ultimately we hear it. Take Carlin's seven words, and then read them: "shit," "piss," fuck," "cunt," "cocksucker," "motherfucker," and "tits." Recalling the notion that sound drives words, in many instances those words that we haphazardly fling about may sound even more effectual when leaping off the page. Without even fully recognizing this, this may be one reason why editors are still squeamish about printing them in their newspapers.

With the liberation of language in so many other sectors, and even in a good deal of journalism itself, some columnists are growing more impatient with the inhibitive rules by which they must discreetly play. Regarding the April 2011 opening of *The Motherfucker With the Hat*,

Times critic Ben Brantley opened his review thusly: "The play that dare not speak its name turns out to have a lot to say. Stephen Adly Guirgis's vibrant and surprisingly serious new comedy opened on Monday night at the Gerald Schoenfeld Theater under a title that cannot be printed in most daily newspapers or mentioned on network television." During the course of his review, he openly bemoans the fact that he must not mention the play's title: "This is vexing for those of us who would like to extol the virtues of 'The _____ With the Hat,' at least in public." He prudently refers to it as the "Hat," much as a superstitious actor finds safety under the umbrella of the "The Scottish Play" for *Macbeth*. Unlike other *Times* writers who ardently defend the newspaper's wholesome front, Brantley makes his feelings of being stifled very clear: "But I'll admit that upon first hearing the name of his play, I thought irritably, 'How the ___ am I going to write about it?' As you see, I have already devoted much space-consuming ink to my quandary." Another New York paper, *Daily News*, went a step further and boldly referred to the play as "The Mother f—with the Hat" in its review. Both the *Wall Street Journal* and *New York Post* reviewed it with the official Broadway title, "The Motherf**ker with the Hat." Interestingly, it was only the *Times* critic who openly caviled over the expurgation, while Terry Teachout just alluded to its unprintability in the *WSJ* review: "Don't let the stupid title put you off. If you do, you'll miss one of the best new plays to come to Broadway in ages."

Clearly, the question here is, "What is newsworthy?" During an international tour spanning five continents, the singer Madonna opened every show with the salutation, "Fuck you, motherfuckers!" Newsworthy? If so, do you couch it in asterisks—and just how many? Few, particularly in the world of journalism, would deny that an incident involving a president caught calling someone a "major-league asshole" is not newsworthy—as evidenced by George W. Bush's captured remarks to Vice President Dick Cheney about then *New York Times* columnist Adam Clyner. The *Washington Post* felt the need to report the matter but posited a substitution for the word in question, a vulgar euphemism for a rectal aperture," which Melvin Lasky said "sounded even more explicit." (Think of Nixon's peculiar use of the word "fornicating" for "fucking.") What followed was copious, and somewhat ludicrous, discourse among various parties if the word was "obscene," "profane," or merely "vulgar." *Times* editor Al Siegal nit-pickingly had this to say, "Folks, if we refer to it again, let's call Bush's word a vulgarity, not an obscenity. It has nothing to do with sex. Nor is it profane, having nothing to do with religion or the deity."

Then there is indeed sex. Sex is openly and indiscriminately referenced everywhere, and this has put traditional newspapers in quite a bind. When sexual activity among well-known personages was judiciously kept behind closed doors, the lives of actors, politicians, and sports personalities were off-limits to the media. For example, stories of Babe Ruth tearing up motel rooms with several women at a pop were considered damaging to his heroic and inspiring image, and they remained scuttlebutt rather than front-page news. During his life, no one dared to report the alleged affairs of the great Bambino in a major newspaper. He was even said to have the nickname the "Sultan of Twat." Today, however, anyone with a name is target for the media. Bill Clinton, Eliot Spitzer, Tiger Woods, Alex Rodriguez, Reverend Ted Haggard, Michael Vick, Clarence Thomas, and Mark Sanford are but a few public figures who have been publicly taken to task for their words and actions. Then there are the celebs: Madonna, Hugh Grant, Pam Anderson, Paris Hilton, Jude Law, and on and on. The tabloids may have a field day with the stories, but major newspapers attempting to retain some degree of journalistic integrity must devise ways to circumspectly report events that their readers are clamoring to learn about. The more famous the celebrity, the more impact an indiscretion will have upon an audience.

If an event is deemed as newsworthy, however, just how far can you go in reporting it without becoming either prurient or obscure?

Just what details should a journalist report about the affair in the Oval Office between Monica Lewinsky and Bill Clinton and references to cigars without sounding like a good joke that was stopped right before the punch line? Once Tiger Woods's infidelities were made known, the Internet was rife with jokes about him as well as with nude photos of one of his mistresses. In some respects this unofficial other news medium, the Web, spared papers like the *Times* from elaborating since others had done it for them. The *Times* could report the affair, knowing that readers would indeed have enough other information to be reading between the lines. On the other hand, when juicy specifics are not already available to the public, papers steeped in vigilant prudence must decide what to print to keep their stories fully informative and credible.

In a rare exception after the fact, the *Times* did allow an expletive to go undeleted in a follow-up article to a previous column from November 10, 2008, about an insult Jesse Jackson railed at President Obama. The initial piece detailed the ensuing controversy and Jackson's apology for what the newspaper called his "critical and crude" remarks, which included the bitter charge that Obama was "talking down to black people." But it left readers completely in the dark about the crude part. Clark Hoyt in his column of three days later addressed the actual quote, "I want to cut his nuts off," adding in parentheses, "The *Times* agreed to an exception to its decision for this column because what he said is central to this discussion." As an aside, the *Washington Post* said Jackson suggested "that he wanted to castrate the presumptive Democratic presidential nominee," and they provided a Web site video link, which the *Times* did not. Meanwhile, the *L.A. Times* and *Chicago Tribune* cited the quote in full, but once again the *New York Post* came out on top by putting the single presumably offending word on its front page as a huge headline. Nevertheless, the *Times* is getting a bit brassier, as is evidenced by an answer in a crossword puzzle that raised some eyebrows in the puzzler community: the answer to 42 down, "What do I care?" was "screw it."

Hoyt cited the *Times* justification for the "nuts" omission: "Paul Winfield, news editor at *The Times*, said he and Chuck Strum, an associate managing editor, made the call to, effectively, bleep Jackson's comments. Winfield said the remark about talking down to black people was what seemed newsworthy to him, while the vulgarity did not seem important enough to make an exception to stringent *Times* standards." The paper admits that choosing when to print or omit a word or phrase can be rather dicey because it neither wants to be a holdout against modern culture nor at the forefront of defining new standards of what is acceptable. "We don't want to cheapen ourselves," said Craig Whitney, the standards editor of the *Times*. "But we don't want to be so prissy we're out of touch." David Remnick, the editor of *The New Yorker*, voiced the more open-minded approach his magazine had for printing the facts when he said, "People use these words in everyday speech. Why should we editors become so decorous and want to protect our readers from them? If a vice president uses a profanity to describe a senator, why should we sanitize his expression?"

David Remnick evidently had an entirely different set of standards than other *New Yorker* editors. It has been recorded that Maxwell Perkins wrote letters to Ernest Hemingway asking him to tone down his language, and author Harold Brodkey used to tell the tale of how legendary editor William Shawn handled his use of a four-letter word: "It's up to you, Shawn said, but would you rather be remembered for your story or the first use of that word in this magazine?" Brodkey nixed the offending expletive. In a bit of bawdy sleuthing, Elon Green published a list of expletives and other sundry taboo words first used by the *New Yorker* in an article for the Awl Web site. From "anal" (printed in 1994) to "vagina" (1995), the A to V list includes "blowjob (2003)," "douchebag (2004)," pussy (1993)," and, of course "fuck," which was used by Calvin Trillin in his "American Chronicles: I've Got Problems":

"Goddamn fuckin' Jews!" Kirk shouted. "They destroyed everything I ever worked for!"

The *Times* proceeds slowly, and with great caution, but it does proceed. Mencken pointed out that the newspapers preferred euphemisms like "social disease" or the ridiculously condescending "vice disease" in lieu of syphilis, venereal disease, or gonorrhea, and that as late as the 1930s the *Times* was still using "blood disease." One might expect to find a more open approach to language in the Sunday language column itself, but even the *Times* near-legendary William Safire held his respectable ground. Few writers could have managed to compose scintillating pieces on the phrases "the shit hit the fan" or "cover your ass" without once mentioning the words "shit" or "ass." Safire did employ a cornucopia of euphemisms for the latter, including "butt," "keister," and "tail"—although he skipped "*derrière*," which would also have been acceptable, since the *Times* was publishing the word as early as 1935. Mencken recounts an advertisement for Bonwit Teller: "'What can I wear that will make me flat enough for the new suits?' This question is most frequently asked by women who have large *derrières*." Let us recall Lenny Bruce's cynical solution mentioned earlier: "*Gluteus maximus* . . . That's alright, that's clean, ass with class, I'll buy it . . . **Clean to you, schmuck, but dirty to the Latins!**" In this case the *Times* might literally beg us to "pardon their French."

Burton Caine, a law professor at Temple University, wrote to protest what he saw as hypocrisy in the newspaper's coverage of the death of George Carlin, when Safire credited Carlin for having performed "a perverse kind of linguistic service" by reducing the shock value of the seven words. Naturally, Safire went nowhere near naming or describing any of those words. Caine said, "It is wrong to praise expression and refuse to print the words." In another instance, Safire did not mention the title of the 1987 film *Sammy and Rosie Get Laid* in a column referencing the movie, because he believed he was writing for a "family trade"—meanwhile adding the seemingly contradictory afterthought that, "besides, it is more titillating to ostentatiously avoid the slang term." Had it been half a century earlier, one wonders if he would have used a milder surrogate for "titillating. Yet for all of its verbal juggling and euphemizing around the words "shit," "ass," and "laid," the *Times* has since allowed them to be printed in its pages on numerous occasions. It would appear that if euphemism is a harbinger of other things to come, the *Times* occasional substitution of "futz" and "futzing around" for the "F-word" may be an indication that the writing is on the wall.

6

YOU'VE GOT TO BE CAREFULLY TAUGHT

"They fuck you up, your mum and dad."
—Philip Larkin, "This Be the Verse"

"Fuck the children!"
—George Carlin

Growing up in the late 1950s I was naive enough to believe that adults did not curse. In fact, like so many other kids back then, I even thought that they did not know how. No, not my parents! I recall an incident one evening in our tiny Queens apartment over a Laundromat when my folks were hosting a party. There I was, a second-grader serenely playing with my soldiers in a corner of the living room when I overheard my father's friend Pat say to him, "Ha, ha! Grand pricks." He was referring to a bottle of some, no doubt rotgut, cognac. No, it could not be, I thought to myself. How could adults know that word? After all, up until then I had never heard anyone older than a teenager use it. Later, I snuck a peek at the bottle and read the words "Grand Prix." I wasn't precocious enough to know what that meant, but I sure as hell knew that this was not how you spell "pricks." My safety returned.

It is to my Uncle Don that I reserve the proper thanks for finally enlightening me and straightening out the matter. It was a summer Sunday of the same year, and I had recently made my First Holy Communion. As a good little Catholic boy back then, I knew that I would be cast into hell if I did not go to mass, even if my aunt and uncle did not care to join me. He reluctantly dressed and dropped me off. Later, when he came to pick me up, the front of the church was lined with double-parked, oversized sedans—undoubtedly with other disgruntled uncles picking up their nephews. After piling into the big, silver Caddy, Uncle Don stepped on the accelerator, but immediately slammed on the brakes as someone pulled out in front of him. At that moment he let out an ear-searing barrage that I can still hear today: "You fucking son-of-a-bitch-and-bastard! Why don't you watch where you're goin'?!" The reply was less intriguing but no less illuminating, "Fuck you, you dumb shithead!" I was a quick study, and as mortified as I was, still digesting the sacrament, it was right then and there I perceived that adults did indeed know how to curse—and pretty darned well. I also realized that I had better watch it, because if I swore, they would know what I was really saying. This was no longer an arcane schoolyard argot. It was the language of the real world. The incident also informed me that just as we kids were holding our tongues in front of our elders, they were likewise holding their tongues in front of us. Could adults be as cool as kids?

This self-censorship is no longer the rule. Meander through a large shopping mall during a busy holiday season and expect to hear parents randomly swear before their children as never before. Sometimes when a very young child first repeats one of those cuss words that his folks have flung about, there is a mixture of amusement and dread: amusement that a four-year-old has just said "shit" and dread that he will say it again—and in front of company. Children instinctively and innocently follow our examples, good and bad, and after we attempt to redress their swearing they will undoubtedly look at us in puzzlement.

If we said it, why can't they? After a child repeated something her mother said, I overheard the mom tell her daughter, "We don't say those words." "No?" the child may have wondered. "But we just did." It may not help that parents can be hypocritical when it comes to swearing. Nearly two-thirds of the adults surveyed who had rules about their children swearing at home found that they broke their own rules on a regular basis. This sends children a mixed, confusing message about swearing and when and if it's appropriate.

Timothy Jay contends that overhearing other people casually swearing may prove harmless, and while there may be no direct harm as a result of children hearing their parents occasional swear, "exposure to conversational swearing could communicate to the child that offensive speech is acceptable in all contexts." He further elaborates that children may then go on to copy their parents swearing outside the home where they won't be punished for doing so. "The issue here is not that harm comes from exposure to arbitrarily determined offensive words, but that harm may be the product of not clearly defining speech standards for children."

So, while parents may indeed "give a shit" about what their kids say in public, they apparently may not have given enough of one early on to curtail their own instigation of it. But it's much too late. The kids know, and they know that we know. Just the fact that kids can see that TV and films are rated on the basis of language should tell us that they—unlike me at the age of eight—are fully aware of the universal hierarchy of dirty words in everyone's employ. The child may not know the full sense of a word or phrase, but he does know the word or phrase. You may not know how to make General Tso's chicken, but you still can order it. And let us not forget that kids are immensely creative, too. For the child who learns the word "pee-pee" for something notably distasteful, it is not a great leap for him to call another child a "pee-pee head," which is clearly the younger brother of the more adult "shithead." Here is another region of language where the human mind, even in its earliest years, is far beyond that of computers. Foul-O-Matic is an insult and foul-language generator that boasts the possibility of more than 10 million possible combinations. Here are two: "Spastic toe baller" and "Flip-flopping poop tranny." The kids win out on this one, I would say.

Children will also adapt their own jargon to the situations and objects with which they are familiar. For example, diarrhea has become "Mountain Doo," "wet fart," the "Hershey squirts," and "mud butt." But we have all been there, haven't we? Back in the 1960s Lenny Bruce commented on the coy reticence of certain adults for saying the word "toilet" in mixed company. He pointed out that people would euphemistically ask for the "little boy's room" or the "little girl's room," and he suggested going a step further and be completely childish and ask for the "tinkle-dinkle-ha-ha room."

Short of complete abstinence, this puerile substitution is often suggested for parents using cuss words in front of their young kids, because—and let's face it—outbursts are inevitable, and children will mimic their folks. "That's just language learning. These words have no special status as taboo words," says Paul Bloom, Ph.D., of Yale University. "Learning they're taboo words is a later step." Using double entendre is another alternative. It may be a sign of sheer cleverness, but it also can be a means of protection. Although a phrase is straightforward on one level, the second meaning is less so, and often couches something inappropriate or risqué. Most adults understand that Bessie Smith wasn't looking for a coffee sweetener when she sang "I want a little sugar in my bowl." The abysmal children's film *The Cat in the Hat* received a PG rating for its use of double entendre, even though most kids would be oblivious to them. For example, when the cat threatens a dog with a garden hoe, and refers to the implement as a "dirty hoe." Perhaps they were there to amuse the parents while sitting through children's flick. In the 1970s series *Are You Being Served?* the character Mrs. Slocombe quite innocently referred to her cat as her "pussy," and the show's writers toyed with her naiveté: "My pussy got soakin' wet. I had to dry it out in front of the fire before I left."

A child might find the latter funny simply because of the visual image of a squirming cat being dried out, but the older viewer would be expected to detect the innuendo. Also, playing on the naiveté of other individuals seems to be quite appealing to some pranksters. A young woman in the rude film *Porky's* (1982) is completely unaware of what she is implying when she is suckered into saying "Phone call for Mike Hunt. Has anyone seen Mike Hunt?" Even the family store Kmart plays on the last example, as we shall soon see. On the other side of the pond, as it were, the spate of British *Carry On* comedies were notorious for double entendre, and they continually played on the audience's ability to listen between the lines. Here are two examples: "Should this Columbus have a route, I would like to get my hands on it" (from *Carry On Columbus*) and "He was one of the biggest bull shippers in the business" (from *Carry On Cruising*, a title you might easily mistake for *Carry On Cursing*). In what Jonathon Green calls the "Nothing New under the Sun Department," he points out that the Brits were no strangers to this punning. He gives the example of the 1731 *The Glass Window, or Bog-House Miscellany*: Here's a Health to Mich. Hunt, / And to Mich. Hunt's Breeches; / And why may not I scratch Mich. Hunt, / When Mich. Hunt itches.

While the intention may be to get a prurient notion across to a certain audience, the sentiment will go unnoticed by others. Shakespeare freely and openly culled from the well of pre- and Reformation swearing, as in "Thou whoreson, senseless villain" or, when using that uniquely English swear, "bloody," "Butchers and villains, bloody cannibals." Ashley Montagu devotes an entire chapter to Shakespeare's conspicuous oaths, but the Bard seemed to be more cautious using blatantly unacceptable language—not that he was not averse to alluding to it:

HAMLET: Lady, shall I lie in your lap?

OPHELIA: No, my lord.

HAMLET: I mean, my head upon your lap?

OPHELIA: Ay, my lord.

HAMLET: Do you think I meant country matters?

The key here, of course, is the phonetic similarity of innocuous words to salacious ones. From Shakespeare's Mercutio saying "'Tis no less, I tell you; for the bawdy hand of the dial is now upon the prick of noon" to AC/DC's line from "Big Balls," "Some balls are held for charity, and some for fancy dress. But when they're held for pleasure, they're the balls that I like best," people have played the game throughout history. As we saw with the *Carry On* quotes, if certain words are not specifically spoken directly, their context is often implied through innuendo, sparing the ingenuous listener. Mae West was famous for her quips: "I'm the kinda girl who works for Paramount by day, and Fox all night," or "I feel like a million tonight—but only one at a time." In other instances the context was apparent, but the words were so familiar in their original meaning that they would be taken by audience members and censors for something else. When Cary Grant was questioned why he was wearing a woman's nightgown in *Bringing Up Baby*, he shouted, "Because I've suddenly gone gay!" "Gay," of course, was predominantly used as bright and lively until fairly recently. Fred Astaire's film *The Gay Divorce* had nothing to do with a same-sex disagreement. Today, with "gay" having entered our language as a particular reference to sexual orientation, Grant's response would be obvious to anyone over the age of ten—or, maybe four.

By the same token, a child watching reruns of the *Flintstones* might have a most peculiar reaction to hearing the line from the title song "We'll have a gay old time." The *Flintstones* had no intention of espousing the word "gay" as a gender preference just as *The Simpsons* did not employ "suck" in sexual terms. Both words evolved, but if the meaning of "gay" intensified in its scope, the latter, "suck," was neutered. And just as youngsters from the 1950s and 1960s would have understood the word "gay" as a variant of happy, present-day kids understand "suck" to mean crummy. For kids watching *Beavis and Butt-Head*, a cornucopia of language that would have sent an earlier generation to bed without supper was at their disposal. When Beavis consumes too much of caffeine or sugar, he transforms into his hyperactive alter ego, Cornholio. In other instances Principal McVicker is referred to as "McDicker." The Beatles are called "asswipes." And, apart from their clearly suggestive names—to adults, anyway—there are comments like Beavis's quip, "Since everyone in England's a wuss, I could go around kicking everybody's ass and then I would be the only person that's not a wussy there." "Kicking ass" is apparently suitable for a TV14 audience, but a no-no if uttered by the president. As for "wuss," even presidents must draw the line somewhere.

With a proliferation of "asswipes," "bungholes," shlongs," and "sucks" on television, the medium has contributed significantly to the jargon of America's youth, but for all of its faults, television is hardly the Big Bad Wolf it is made out to be. This is because children aren't just learning swear words from the television they watch as much as they are from picking it up from the cursing they hear everywhere they go. You may not want to agree with him, but Timothy Jay's careful studies have led him to conclude: "We find their swearing really takes off between (ages) three and four." By the time kids go to school, they're saying the potential words that watchdog agencies and well-intentioned parents are trying to protect them from on television. TV is often merely reiterating, albeit with embellishments, what they already know. Perhaps a teen may have "picked it up on the street," as we used to say, but the chances are that a four-year-old learned the four-letter words from somebody he knew.

We have noted earlier that toddlers, not yet having the ability to speak, will cry as an emotional outlet, with the crying growing to accommodate the needs of the situation. Montagu observed that when a child reaches adolescence, crying and childish naughtiness are abandoned for the more manly forms of conduct; where one formerly wept, one now swears." He goes on to cite this example from an old *Punch* cartoon:

OLD LADY: Why are you crying, little boy?
LITTLE BOY: Because I bea'nt old enough to swear.

"Obscenity is a sure ticket to adulthood," says Paul Bloom. Or, in the very least, it is a way for teenagers to perceive that they sound older. On the other hand, if the parent indifferently swears, the child may not even recognize the gravity it might imply for others, and this creates a double standard not necessarily fathomed by the child. To repeat, it sends a mixed, confusing message about swearing and when it's appropriate. The award-winning HBO series *The Sopranos* is rife with cursory cursing; so much so that when young A. J. Soprano finds out that his grandmother won't be coming over, he protests, "So what? So no fuckin' ziti now?" Bear in mind that he says this in front of his parents and the parish priest—all of whom take umbrage at the remark. For all intents and purposes, A. J. may not have fully understood exactly why his casual remark invoked such displeasure. After all, he was a boy growing into manhood, and if it was acceptable for his tough-talking father and his cronies, why wasn't it so for him? "As soon as kids can speak, they're using swear words," says Jay. "That doesn't mean they know what adults know, but they do repeat the words they hear."

The problem here is that some parents simply do not want to address the issue of why they themselves swear, and, subsequently, they do not, or perhaps even cannot, realistically explicate the child's obscenities. There is the joke about the young twin boys who grew up swearing like sailors. The language was once cute, but then it was obviously becoming quite exasperating. The mother mentioned this to the father, and the latter said that he would correct the problem. At dinner the first twin asked, "Hey, pop, please pass the fuckin' potatoes." With that, the father rose from his chair and walloped the kid. Turning to the other twin, he inquired, "And what do *you* want?" To this the boy nervously replied, "I don't know what I want, but I know I don't want those fuckin' potatoes." Once again we return to the reliance upon explaining context, because without it, these words are meaningless.

At some point, parents realize that their child does have a lexicon of swear words at his or her command, and they can face it or ignore it. One of the most foolish suggestions out there is to substitute specific words or make up your own phrases like "son of a biscuit." Here are some samples from *Cuss Control*:

That's a bunch of Bolshevik.

I don't give a pumpernickel.

You Fudrucker.

The latter is the most humorous, as an early use of fud was for pubic hair. Jonathon Green cites Robert Burns' 1786 *Jolly Beggars*: They scarcely left to coer their fuds.

Other people recommend direct substitutions such as "flip," "fleck," "feck," and "fudge," but by far my favorite is the one Pat Boone uses when things go amiss: "Boone!" And yet, isn't that all missing the point? Remember Carlin's, "You can't fool me, 'shoot' is just 'shit' with a double O." In these instances, the words may be gone, but the context remains, making the surrogate words just as meaningful as the ones they replaced. I never heard my mother swear, but she would say things like "Stop futzing around," much to the consternation and head-shaking of my father. Wise man that he was, he knew that this substitution was all just "bull-shipping." Not that he was innocent of euphemizing, as he was wont to utter the likes of "He's a big pain in the foot" and "Go blow it out your nose." Then there was Sarah

Palin, who in response to hearing about a government official's Web site predicting and advocating a race war, commented on Facebook, "Unflippingbelievable!"

There is also the reverse—starting with an entirely innocent context and enticing the listener to impose his own reformulation. Take the hilarious Kmart advertisement for free shipping. A slightly befuddled fellow quizzically replies to a salesman, "Ship my pants, right here?" From there, the rest of his family happily join him in the fact that they can "ship their pants." The context is entirely innocent, but the twelve-year-old in all of us cannot possibly avoid making a connection to "shitting ones pants." Kmart concludes with the risible, "Want to ship your pants too? Can't find what you're looking for in store, a sales associate can find it on Kmart.com and ship it to you for free!" And, that they will do it for free only compounds the farcical felony. More recently, the big box behemoth has come out with another "Ship My Pants" ad for the holidays, this one featuring Charles Dickens' "A Christmas Carol." It's called "Ship My Trousers." Let us admit it: direct swearing, or even swearing by implication, can be appealing. Whether it's the San Diego clothier Mudafuga or the Effen vodka company, there is evidently some wicked pleasure at appearing risqué. Mencken cited philosopher and political theorist Herbert Spencer in this regard: "Herbert Spencer's objection to swearing, of which much has been made by moralists, was not an objection to its sinfulness but an objection to its charm. In brief, he feared comfort, satisfaction, joy." It is only fitting that a book titled *The Joy of Swearing* (by M. Hunt and Allison Maloney) should have appeared in print in the first decade of the new millennium.

Other stalwart individuals have taken the business to heart and have actually initiated preventative measures to curtail profanity. It made national news in June of 2012 when residents in a town of Middleborough, Massachusetts, a sleepy little burb just outside Boston, voted to make the foul-mouthed pay fines for swearing in public. At a town meeting, residents voted 183–50 to approve a proposal from the police chief to impose a $20 fine on public profanity. Bear in mind that Middleborough is only thirty-eight miles from Boston and Fenway Park, where Red Sox fans bestowed a profane nickname on New York Yankee Bucky Dent after the light-hitting shortstop homered in the seventh inning of a tiebreaker game in 1978. Call him Bucky "Bleeping" Dent in Middleborough and it will cost you $20. Officials insisted that the proposal was not intended to censor casual or private conversations, but instead to crack down on loud, profanity-laden language used by teens and other young people in the downtown area and public parks. Oh those kids—I wonder where they learned it.

If anything, it is a far better thing to explain to your kids what is being said than simply inexplicably forbidding it. Children are getting a raw deal if they are not treated like the growing and developing individuals they are. Ostensibly, to protect our children's innocence, the religious right and other censorial groups want to prevent us from making our own choices about what to watch or say. We hear it continually that we must protect the children—always the children. It is understandable then why George Carlin said, "Fuck the children!" What he meant was that there are people out there who want to take away your adult right to view shows like *Deadwood* because it is bad for children. Well, it's not meant for the kids, just as *Alvin and the Chipmunks: Chip-Wrecked* may not be meant for us. As adults we do not need to cater all of our entertainment choices to children. Discretion is advisable, but blind censorship is not, particularly in an era when kids can be far more vulgar that adults. Understanding and dialog are paramount.

Despite protests from parent groups, and so on, however, the entertainment business appears to have no difficulty with adults swearing in films in front of children. Billy-Bob Thornton indiscriminately throws "fuck" around throughout the film *Bad Santa*, often within the ears of kids. With one child on his lap he growls at an inquisitive tyke with, "Don't fuck with my beard." Or, when asked in wide-eyed awe if he was Santa, Thornton acerbically snorted, "No, I'm a fucking accountant. This is a fashion statement." In effect, he was puncturing a revered myth: "No, Virginia. There is no fucking Santa Claus." The grown-ups were finally getting even with the sweet fallacies foisted upon them in childhood, and even if it was presented in a humorous fashion, or because it was indeed presented in a humorous fashion, they were not about to spare the present generation of impressionable youths from the lie. Sorry, Virginia.

It is becoming more prevalent that if the kids can hear it, they can say it, and the list of movies with kids swearing is growing. "Fuck you, Miss Daisy," spouted by the feisty foul-mouthed preteen Ronnie in 2008's *Role Models* may never attain the celebrity of "Frankly, my dear, I don't give a damn," but the flurry of kiddy cussing had its viewers laughing in the aisles, or as one blogger put it, "ROMAPIMP" (which is to say, rolling on my ass, pissing in my pants). A more circumspect adult in the same film spells out S-H-I-T-T-Y in front of a mother and her son, to which the mother snaps, "He *can* spell!" Other films like *Superbad*, *Kids*, *Kickass*, and *Big Daddy* are just a sampling of films that revel in the torrents of profanity from the "mouths of babes." Even that very familiar phrase implies something else if you are looking for it. Could it be that adult viewers find these films to be hilarious in part because they are transferring their own rebellious inner child at the stupid adults who repressed them in their youth? And let us not forget that adult screenwriters are the ones putting these words into the mouths of babes. Adults are patently aiding and abetting kids in their rebellion against the norms and conventions of society. Whereas Cee Lo Green's "Fuck You!" may be taken one way as pure audio, the video presents an even greater defiance since he has a teen lip-syncing to his lyrics "Fuck you, and fuck her too." Child is father to the man, and man is he pissed off! Legman approaches it a bit more clinically:

"These jokes are the revenge of the child who has grown up, and can now tell his own stories. The final and pointed indictment puts the finger

on the purulent seat of the disease: Lying and cruelty to children, and the abnormalization to suit the parents' and society's sick needs."

Legman takes the approach to the extreme, but parental needs need not be so truculent. Sometimes adults just want a break. Take the example of the stereotypical image of that cuddly, little "bundle of joy"—the Gerber baby, if you will. As much as parents would like to endorse that delightful image, most parents of newborns are at some time or another besieged by the reality of decibel-shattering colicky or teething babe who can wail like a banshee with apoplexy. As yet incapable of understanding any consolation we might offer, we comfortingly croon to the nipper or rock the child in our arms in the hope of the onset of sleep—his and ours. Quite naturally, the babe will grow, as most do, into that toddler who can understand our words and, in turn, speak to us; usually with such phrases as "I'm thirsty," "I'm scared of the monster under my bed," or "Tell me another story." It is then time for the beleaguered parents to guard their language against what they really want to say, which just happens to be the title of the wildly successful nonchildren's bedtime story: *Go the Fuck to Sleep.* To cite one verse:

> *The eagles who soar through the sky are at rest,*
> *And the creatures who crawl, run and creep.*
> *I know you're not thirsty. That's bullshit. Stop lying.*
> *Lie the fuck down, my darling, and sleep.*

The author, Adam Mansbach, initially penned the book as a joke, undoubtedly as a lament of his own trials and ordeals with an insomniac child. Evidently his plight was not a singular one, since the book skyrocketed on Amazon before publication and has been translated into at least twelve languages. Not having seen all of those other versions, it will be interesting to read how our singular nonsexual "fuck" will be rendered. At least in French it is *Dors et fais pas chier!*

(Go to sleep, and don't give me shit!). In any language, it is the implied sentiment of parental rebellion that will carry the import, and not any particular word. While ostensibly not a book directly for kids, *Go the Fuck to Sleep* stands as an emotional outlet for the discommoded adult (an outlet that will one day no doubt be inherited by the young adult-to-be). Mansbach comments, "It captures the frustration of being in a room with a kid and feeling like you may actually never leave that room again, that you may spend the rest of your life in that dark room, trying to get your kid to go to sleep."

The cheeky little volume quickly became so popular that Samuel L. Jackson was approached by his agent to narrate the book for Audible. Before the actual recitation begins, Jackson—who is no stranger to the diverse species of four-letter words—shares his own exasperating experiences trying to get his daughter to go to sleep. Meanwhile, there is a video of the *real* Werner Herzog reading it at a book party at the New York Public Library in June of 2011. I wonder, though, as a bestseller for adults, will some parents hide it from their kids? If so, can you imagine the young boy's surprise when, while hunting through his father's closet for hidden smut, he happens upon a well-worn copy of *Go the Fuck to Sleep* secreted away between the socks and undies. It may not stay a secret for long, however, as Fox 2000 has purchased the movie rights.

For those on either side of the generation gap, it is all a fight for power. Unlike the hypothetical "battle of the sexes," however, where men and women cannot change sides (except perhaps in cases of transgendering), children will become adults. The secret was out long ago that children feel that it is their province to be contrary to acceptable behavior, from innocuous swearing and shirking to detrimental drug abuse and promiscuity. Moreover, as Slavoj Žižek explains, a teenager "cannot bear the idea that his mother could be doing something similar." On the other side of the battlefield, the adult takes umbrage in the belief that he or she must traipse the straight and narrow, which makes an irreverent book like *Go the Fuck to Sleep* so appealing.

Youngsters can also be rebellious in the opposite way, by using an adult's talk of sex to harass him. This can be seen in the number of court cases where teens have "turned in" their teachers for speaking indecent language aloud. Timothy Jay cites several examples, and one will suffice here. In the court case that was cited as *Keefe v. Geanakos*, an English teacher had brought in an article from the *Atlantic* for the class to read and discuss. The article, which addressed the issue of protest and dissent in America, contained the word "motherfucker." The irony here is that the entire class was undoubtedly familiar with the word on their own terms and in their own turf, and some may have even invoked it to verbally abuse a teacher. However, when the teacher applied it here, even though it was in an educational context, the students attempted to take down a figure of power. They were not offended by the word as much as they were resorting to it as ammunition in an act of rebellion to the authority he represented. Parents are naturally disposed to what their kids say to them about what negatively happened in school, and if the teacher swore, he or she should be reprimanded, if not dismissed. As Jay explained, adults who hear rumors should get the facts before they pass judgments. A further irony is that so many parents rely upon teachers to educate their children regarding sex, and, as a result, the parents are happily spared the onus of having to do it themselves at home.

To this end, Jay published *What to Do When Your Students Talk Dirty*, a handy guidebook of sorts "to provide teachers with methods and strategies to reduce the use of cursing at school." For example, what do you say to a student who, when questioned why she moved to another part of the room, says, "Because that guy in front of me smells like dog crap"? Obviously you allow her to move (because who wants to sit behind someone who smells like "dog crap"), but you should also tell the student that "she should refer to the student in front of her as having a foul odor or a bad smell. Remind her that the word 'crap' is vulgar and that some more polite term be substituted." Wise advice as this may be, I think the one with the most urgent problem is the stinky kid. More and more, teachers are being given broad latitude in deciding when and how to control their students' language. The attorney Ira Robbins warns of the danger attached to this responsibility: "With this power comes an obligation to safeguard the First Amendment rights of young people, because the vigilant protection of constitutional freedoms is nowhere more vital than in the community of American schools." This is far more generous than a law instituted by British Parliament in the seventeenth century, imposing the death penalty on children who used profanity against their parents.

So, presumably kids can handle swearing—and apparently much more. Bill Maher in his predictably flip manner assessed the current situation of children's awareness of adult themes by recalling an article he had read that contended that kids were bored with porn: "Kids are bored with porn? Why, kids in China are starving for it." Undeniably, swearing is part and parcel of our evolving language as a reflection of the culture in which we live. To deny that and feign that our children's vocabularies are a reflection of the same world in which we live is hypocrisy. If you are serious or concerned about the development of your child, you should heed the words of Stephen Sondheim from his play *Into the Woods*:

> *Careful the things you say*
> *Children will listen.*
> *Careful the things you do,*
> *Children will see.*
> *And learn.*

7

YOU HAVE THE WORDS, MY DEAR, BUT I'M AFRAID YOU'LL NEVER MASTER THE TUNE

"Let's spend the night together"
—The Rolling Stones

"Let's spend some time together"
—The Rolling Stones (as sung on the *The Ed Sullivan Show*, 1967)

So far, all reference to swearing in print, television, film, and music has been interwoven. Music, however, deserves its own chapter, because while swearing can be found in all media, it seems to have its own rules and ways of breaking them. For example, on any given Saturday evening a broad spectrum of society may go to the multiplex in the mall, where ten or more different films may be showing. Some of the flicks will appeal only to certain moviegoers, and other moviegoers would rather eat bees than watch those films. Chris Rock offered a rationale for that in a *Times* interview: "No film critic's going to say it, but 'Madagascar 3' is better than 'The Artist,' and it's better because it makes people feel better." Still, while some of the recent films have included "adult language," the swearing in the *King's Speech* (2010) was markedly different from that in *South Park: Bigger, Longer & Uncut.* Although censorship has hounded the music business throughout the last century, out-and-out swearing has been mostly relegated to rock and rap, and, therefore, to a very select, and generally younger, audience. Being such, music is scrutinized with different eyes and different intent than the other more ecumenical media.

In the case of the Rolling Stone's "Let's Spend the Night Together," clearly the culprit of bowdlerization was television and not the music industry, per se; and yet it is telling that music in the 1960s was already being carefully monitored and censored in certain venues of public taste. The song was played on the radio, but certain purveyors of public decency were able to suppress it on TV. Although the Stones also changed the title of their song "Star Fucker" to "Star Star" on their 1973 album *Goats Head Soup*, they did not alter the actual lyrics, as evidenced by the chorus, which repeats "star fucker" over and over.

In fact, the popular music industry has a dramatic record, if you will, of resistance to the demands of authority, and, consequently, it has been the continued target of vilification by governmental agencies and individual moralizing crusaders alike. And popular music shows no sign of surrendering. Witness an article that music critic John Pareles recently wrote in the *New York Times*, "It's *some* kind of milestone: Three of the Top 10 hits on last week's pop music chart have choruses that can't be played uncensored on the radio and won't have their original lyrics quoted in this family newspaper. All three use variations on a familiar, emphatic, percussive four-letter word." Note here again that the *Times* still would not use the word "fuck" in print. Nevertheless, did anyone in the family reading the article think he was referring to anything but "fuck"?

Mr. Pareles pointed out that the word was not only uttered, but is right in the titles of two of the songs. Cee Lo Green's aforementioned song "Fuck You!" was nominated for a Grammy Award, although, perhaps deferring to Prince's nouveau sobriquet, it was referred to as

"The Song Also Known as 'Forget You.'" For those folks who are hearing impaired, and unable to savor the original lyrics, there is a YouTube video featuring a young woman signing the classic song. Bowing to possible propriety, or just hoping to reach a broader market, Pink's self-help power ballad "Fuckin' Perfect" was also released in a cuss-free version, as was Enrique Iglesias's dually titled hit "Tonight (I'm Lovin' You)" and "Tonight (I'm Fuckin' You)." There is something of a sense of schizophrenia here, because the songs indeed have dual personalities but are still rooted in the same source. The FCC-approved versions may appeal to a smaller, oblivious crowd, but these tame renditions are akin to PG movie trailers enticing the audience to buy into the R-rated version. Once in, you are part of a select club, party to the song writer's real intentions. You are also an outlaw against the system. Perhaps there was no better example of this than when Country Joe McDonald led half a million concert goers at Woodstock in his immortal "F-U-C-K cheer." But Cee Lo Green, playing at Madison Square Garden in February 2011, did not even need to sing his "fuck you" refrain. He slyly grinned and held his microphone out to the audience, and thousands of fans sang it out for him. According to Pareles, "Mr. Green had deniability, while the audience got to shout the forbidden word." And they were loving it at that.

From its outset, rock music was deemed rebellious, savage, and even ungodly, and it was also thought to inspire teens to become violent-prone hoodlums with voracious sexual appetites. Just the mention of the term rock 'n' roll provoked controversy because it initially implied the sexual act, which is evident from the manner in which it is used in the title of Tampa Red's "My Daddy Rocks Me with a Steady Roll." As rock began to heat up in the 1950s, it was met with attacks at every turn. Peter Blecha gives a thorough chronicle of censorship in music in his *Taboo Tunes*, and he accounts for most of it due to authority's belief that it was threatening the foundations of a moral society. He quotes one Dr. Braceland, a former psychiatrist-in-chief of Hartford,

Connecticut's Institute of Living, who averred that rock 'n' roll was a "cannibalistic and tribalistic" form of music that was a "dangerous communicable disease with music appealing to adolescent insecurity and driving teenagers to do outlandish things." How that makes teenagers any different from anyone else is beyond me.

All of that aside, those who maintained that rock stirred the animal instincts or incited delinquency, railed primarily against the music itself: the strident chords, the cacophony, the irregular beats, and, of course, its loudness. If rock 'n' roll entered the world as rebellious upstart, it was in its beat that it sounded its cry against the established order. Blecha asserted that rock 'n' roll was a music form in which "the 'beat' is perhaps the most pronounced and defining aspect—the same epithets that had been applied to jazz were transferred wholesale to the new music." Like its forerunner in jazz, rock was associated with drugs, the left, and, of course, blacks. The continued diatribes against early rock often included slurs like "jungle or voodoo music." In the words of one Reverend Riblett, "Rock and roll is the devil's diversion. It has been traced back to jungle drums. . . . The headhunters use the same beat before they go out to hunt heads."

Disparaging the beat as much as they did, they could not fight the innate feeling there is some form of music that soothes the savage breast in all of us. The rhythm has even hoodwinked some of the most twin-left-footed persons to believe that they could dance. Early rock 'n' roll had been lauded and derided, but there was no getting around what everyone was taken with: it was its rhythm and the beat. The great blues singer Muddy Waters famously summed it all up when he said, "You throw away all of them fancy chords—what you got to have is the beat."

That is not to say that themes went unchallenged. "Charlie Brown" by the Coasters was banned by the BBC because they believed it encouraged rebelliousness in school, while Bobby "Boris" Pickett's "Monster Mash" was also banned by the BBC as having offensive subject matter. Still, as for the lyrics themselves, the vocabulary of rock 'n' roll was fairly tame in its early years. Some radio stations dropped rock 'n' roll altogether, denouncing it as "distorted, monotonous, noisy . . . and suggestive," but "suggestive" is hardly demonstrative. Then there are the words, and we have come a long way from the suggestive "My Ding-a-Ling" by Chuck Berry to the unreserved "Let's Get Buck Naked and Fuck" by Ice-T. The explosion of expletives as well as formerly taboo themes led to the creation of the aforementioned Parents Music Resource Center (PMRC) by Tipper Gore, Senator Strom Thurmond's wife, Nancy, Treasury Secretary James Baker's wife, Susan, and a powerful handful of other concerned Washington wives. Ironically, for all of its bluster and its success at sticking its "parental advisory" label on thousands of recordings, the actual prohibition of sales to minors was never legally approved. One reason for the failure of banning sexually suggestive music that might appeal to the "prurient interests" of minors was that operas by Mozart, Wagner, and Verdi could also be deemed offensive. Meanwhile, individual stores, like Wal-Mart and J.C. Penny, may have chosen not to carry "parental advisory" disks on their shelves, but there was still no legal restriction against their sale. Since kids and not their parents were buying albums, the label readily served as a signpost for which recordings had the juiciest lyrics. Furthermore, bands rallied 'round the label and commenced their objections to the new self-appointed censors by penning such songs as "PMRC Can Suck on This," "Censorshit," and "Tipper Gore for Prozac"—which was only one of many songs drubbing the illustrious Ex-Second Lady.

Certainly sexuality is openly touted on albums. With *Purple Rain*, Prince became something of a poster boy for the PMRC, because it was that particular album that Tipper Gore, in a "St. Paul on the road to Damascus" moment singled out as her of epiphany to clean up the smut out there. Prince declaring "We can fuck until the dawn" in "Erotic City," or 2 Live Crew's "We Want Some Pussy" on *2 Live Is What*

We Are are but two examples of songs that enraged conservatives and resulted in fines for radio stations for airing obscenity. The Eurythmics saw their 1984 hit "Sexcrime" banned by a number of radio stations for simply using the words "sex" and "crime" in the same song. As for the radio stations that did play the likes of The Pork Duke's "Makin' Bacon" and "Tight Pussy," Elton Motello's "Jet Boy, Jet Girl" ("I wanna take you round the world"), along with other "novelty" songs such as "Walk with an Erection" and "Penis Envy," they were fined to the tune of thousands of dollars in the hope of discouraging them from "playing risqué music."

The rampage continued however, with 2 Live Crew's album as *Nasty as They Want to Be*, which raised public outcry in numerous states. Part of the objection may have been due to the fact that the sexy lyrics were turning a lot of middle-class white kids into rap fans. The rage for decency, and the persecution of 2 Live Crew came to a head in Broward County, Florida, in March of 1990 when a county circuit judge declared that the album was obscene under Florida's "sale of harmful material" statute. Record dealer Charles Freeman had the dubious honor of being convicted of selling obscenity in the form of the 2 Live Crew album. Although it was a misdemeanor, it was still the first instance of a person being convicted of selling obscene music in the United States. As for 2 Live Crew, they were arrested as well and charged with obscenity for performing their songs in an adults-only club in Hollywood, Florida. They were acquitted, however, but not before watching their album pulled from music stores around the country. As of this writing, *Nasty as they Want to Be* is still a perennial favorite on Amazon.

But further attacks by the FCC, PMRC, and other conservative organizations only fired the rebellious spirit of musicians, and not only First Amendment speech pertaining to sex. In keeping with its antiestablishment heritage, rock, along with its obstreperous new partner, rap, took up the call. Rappers may not have been familiar with

Tom Joad in *The Grapes of Wrath*, who vowed, "Wherever they's a fight so hungry people can eat, I'll be there. Wherever they's a cop beatin' up a guy, I'll be there," but they were well aware of the sentiment. Poverty, discrimination, and police brutality were no strangers to life on the street. And just as conservative groups bigotedly associated jazz and early rock 'n' roll with the "jungle music" of Africa, a prevailing group of white Americans branded rap and hip-hop as "ghetto" music that was undermining the fabric of society. Thanks to the age of modern video recorders, there was no hiding the iniquities of those in power anymore. The brutal police beating of Rodney King in 1991 is perhaps the most infamous encounter to be recorded. Given the spate of songs already aimed at the police's dereliction of duties and the inequities of society, such barbarous incendiary incidents only exacerbated matters.

The Rodney King travesty may have been the first to attract national attention, but it was certainly not an isolated case. That black Americans were already voicing their anger at the police was particularly made apparent in the 1989 release "Fuck Tha Police" from the album *Straight Outta Compton* by N.W.A (Niggers With Attitude). What separated N.W.A from the myriad other groups who had also decried the police's actions was that this band out of California received an unsigned letter of condemnation from the FBI declaring that the Bureau "does not appreciate the song 'Fuck Tha Police.'" Bowing to pressure from the conservative group Focus on the Family, it was the first time in history that the FBI took an official, albeit anonymous stance, against a work of art. Subsequently, and most unintentionally justifying the band's point, they were whisked off the stage in Detroit and escorted to their hotel room where they were held by police for several hours—without being charged. I wonder why?

The most notorious case of all, however, would involve Ice-T's release "Cop Killer" from the 1992 album *Body Count*. Many artists were rightfully enraged by the King affair and wrote songs displaying their ire, but Ice-T's lyrics seemed to have struck a nerve. With the repeated lines of "Fuck the police" and "Cop killer," how could it not?

Police organizations around the nation protested; sixty congressmen along with Dan Quayle and the ever-respectable Lt. Col. Ollie North joined them and wrote letters directly to Time Warner pressuring them to drop the tune. It is not without interest that the thirty-five-thousand member National Black Police Association refused to join the boycott, issuing the statement, "Where were these police groups when the police beat up Rodney King?" Time Warner eventually gave in and dropped the song from the album. As Peter Blecha points out, Time Warner did speak out in Ice-T's defense—after all, they did have a lot of money riding on the popular singer—and claimed that he had a constitutional right to write his music. This lukewarm endorsement only angered Ice-T all the more: "It was always: 'Well, he has the First Amendment right. I don't agree with him, but . . .' *Fuck that!* Back me on the fact that Ice-T has *grounds* to say: Fuck the police.' "Cause the police have been killing his people. . . . The motherfuckers are savage! Say: 'That's why he made the record. He has *grounds* to make it.' *Not* just the right." Nevertheless, the song was the first in American history that was actually banned and withdrawn from public distribution, and it is still technically unavailable for purchase. It is for sale, however, as a used item on several Web sites.

In the springtime, the "hey ding a ding, ding" time of halcyon song, all is well, and the birds in the tree may sing their "dayful of song," so why shouldn't we sing along? Well, as a song, "Cop Killer" is no great loss. Cab drivers from Borneo to Nome will much prefer "My Way." And yet, if ever there was a song that demanded the dictum that I may not agree with what you say, but I will defend to the death your right to say it, it is "Cop Killer." Disdain it, hate it, and vehemently rail against it if you need to, but, for heaven and hell's sake, do not disallow it. Doing so will only set up a standard to prevent you from voicing your opinion in the future. Although I mentioned this Lenny

Bruce quote earlier, I think it bears repeating: "Take away the right to say 'fuck' and you take away the right to say 'fuck the government.'" Right on, Lenny.

Advocates of free speech in music marched into the twenty-first century side by side with those zealots hoping to stifle them. In the war of words, Bruce Springsteen did not need to invoke Ice-T's brand of malediction to incite the ire of the New York Fraternal Order of Police (NYFOP) when he released his song "American Skin" in 2000. Springsteen condemned the killing of Amadou Diallo, who, while reaching for his wallet, was shot an incredible forty-one times by police officers who assumed it was a gun. Without apologizing for the incident, the NYFOP president instead had this to say about Springsteen: "He's turned into some type of fucking dirtbag. He has all these good songs and everything, American flag songs and all that stuff, and now he's a floating fag. You can quote me on that." We just did, pal. That same year, Lynn Cheney went before the Federal Trade Commission holding hearings before the Senate on the proposed regulation of the entertainment industry. Specifically targeting the songs of white rapper Eminem, she ranted, "It is despicable. It is horrible. This is dreadful. This is shameful. This is awful." It would appear that Dick had given her a thesaurus for her birthday.

And then it hit—or, rather, they hit. Al-Qaeda terrorists crashed jet planes into the Twin Towers in downtown Manhattan, and in their wake came a steady stream of extremist neo-conservatism that bordered on fascism. It seemed that radio stations assumed that they were given carte blanche to censor music in order to mollify their listeners' emotions in a time of tragedy. Blecha illustrates the folly of it all in citing the rumor that Clear Channel network blacklisted 158 songs from airtime. Although it was reported that compliance to the list was voluntary, just a few examples will serve to demonstrate its absurdity: "Burning Down the House" by the Talking Heads, "Knockin' on Heaven's Door" by Bob Dylan, "Wipeout" by the Surfaris, along with Sinatra's "New

York, New York," and Peter, Paul & Mary's "Leavin' on a Jet Plane." Of course, if you could ban Simon and Garfunkel's "Bridge Over Troubled Water," it was only a short step to banishing anything that remotely smacked of insurrection. If these examples appear over the top, a station in Texas banned all of Bob Dylan's music in 1968 because they *couldn't* understand the lyrics. The El Paso station was afraid that Dylan might have been swearing, and they pulled the albums as a cautionary measure just in case he was. Prince's 1992 hit "Sexy Motherfucker" was understandable—but "Bridge Over Troubled Water?"

All of the songs by Rage Against the Machine, including "Know Your Enemy" and "Freedom," were also on the list. Perhaps it was a line like "Fuck you, I won't do what you tell me" from "Killing in the Name" that was the cause. In that same period, Secret Service inquiries to the band's Web host intimidated it into taking down the online message board because of anti-Bush statements posted there by fans. The Bush family was keen on attacking musicians even when they were merely voicing their opinions against W. Father Bush "vented his spleen" yet again when he took umbrage over the Dixie Chicks comment that they were embarrassed to come from the same state as his son: "They're on my shit list." No doubt this was a very long list.

Eventually, as the nation found itself in an unjustifiable war in Iraq, support for the Patriot Act and President Bush's decision was gradually greeted with suspicion, and then downright defiance. Public Enemy released "Fight the Power" with the song "Son of a Bush," and other groups followed suit with such songs as "Bushleaguer" by Pearl Jam and "George Bush Is an Asshole" by Wesley Willis. Naturally, these tunes received no airplay on corporate radio leading the *New York Times* to comment, "There are plenty of angry people, many with music-buying demographics. But independent radio stations that once played edgy music have been gobbled up by corporations that control hundreds of stations and have no wish to rock the boat. Corporate ownership has changed what gets played—and who plays it." At least there is satellite radio, gently rocking that boat. John Pareles in his more recent *Times* piece on Cee Lo Green remarked that even if "original lyrics are off-limits to old media, it's clear to everyone that profane versions of the songs are going to be heard. The enforced innocence of broadcasting is no longer a cultural firewall; it's barely an inconvenience."

Then there are musicians themselves. Whether singing about violence in the streets or love between the sheets, artists like Ke$ha, Eminem, Fergie, B.o.B, Lil Wayne, Avril Lavigne, Guns 'N' Roses, Pink, Katy Perry, and Goblin, or contemporary and rock-driven Tony-Award winning Broadway musicals such as *Billy Elliot*, *Spring Awakening*, and *Avenue Q* will keep the "Tipper Sticker" in constant circulation. Since the sticker is a voluntary prohibitive, and not a mandatory one, the 2011 Tony winner *Book of Mormon* does not carry one, which could create quite a shock for those looking for something along the lines of greatest hits of the Mormon Tabernacle Choir. Still, in the words of Edgar Varese, often quoted by the often-censored Frank Zappa, "The present day composer refuses to die!" To further substantiate the all-pervasive grip that the PMRC has had on the record industry, Zappa's *Jazz from Hell* was given a "parental advisory" label. The recording was entirely instrumental without any lyrics whatsoever.

8

WORD ON THE STREET

"There is no such thing as bad language."
—Robert Claiborne, *Our Marvelous Native Tongue*

Street language is predominantly slang, and although swearing may be herded into this fold, this is not a book about slang per se. I defer to the master lexicographer of slang for that (and for so much more), Jonathon Green, for your edification and solo flute playing amusement. Therefore this will be a brief look at street talk in relation to just swearing. Without a doubt, word on the street is open. It would be fair to say that the smaller the town you live in, or the more closely knit your community is, the more personal you will be with your neighbors, be it friendly or hostile. The streets of Boston, New York, and Chicago are havens of anonymity where the urban cave dweller can parade about without fear of someone tapping him on the shoulder and asking him to watch his language. Yes, there is a special rudeness in anonymity, but there is also the superiority in being anonymous and better than your nameless neighbor. Timothy Jay is correct in his conclusion that "the more society shifts away from group cohesion and group effort toward an isolated, individualized lifestyle, the more one can speak and do what one wants without worrying about retaliation."

On the other hand, off the street and in the office, the opposite holds true. The larger the corporation, the more controlled the workplace environment will be, whereas in smaller workplace settings, more liberal attitudes will most likely prevail. Likewise, the business-like settings, safely tucked in concrete and glass towers, will promote a more formal atmosphere, but the closer you are to the street, the closer you are to reality and the language that goes with it.

Despite the throngs of people shuffling up and down the avenues and streets of Manhattan during any given lunch hour, the pairs and trios conversing among themselves tend to be oblivious to the thousands of other people around them. I am reminded of episodes of *Get Smart* where Agent 86 and the Chief sit between the protective "cone of silence" to conceal their conversation, but they end up shouting so that anyone in earshot can hear them. Unless you are a real busybody, however, you will most likely not even pay any attention to what is being said around you. Nevertheless, listening to conversations surely informs us that public swearing is not going away anytime soon. Whether couples are griping between themselves about "the fucking deal that fell through," or someone is solitarily grousing about the "clusterfuck" of midtown traffic, or one guy is deriding another as a "shithead" for stepping on his brand-new Thom McAns, the stressful hassles of everyday life mount up and must be expelled. Between swearing openly on the street and people gabbing on their handless cell phones, it's getting difficult to recognize who has Tourette Syndrome anymore.

Actually, that last remark was said in only half jest. Timothy Jay describes Tourette Syndrome (TS) as a "rare and puzzling neurological disorder characterized by uncontrollable muscular twitches, facial tics, vocalizations, repetitive movements, compulsive touching, and, probably most troublesome in public, uncontrollable cursing, or coprolalia." Tourette sufferers are apt to shout out phrases like "Fuck me up the asshole" or "Dirty miserable motherfucking son of a bitch" in public places. Ironically, it seems that public places tend to bring on the flurry of obscenities. Jay also remarks that "children learn offensive words and then spend the rest of their lives inhibiting them in public. What is interesting is the Touretter's inability to inhibit curse words that normal children *can* inhibit in 'polite' situations." As enigmatic as the disease may be, it is estimated that swearing is produced by the same neurolinguistic mechanisms that all individuals possess, whether or not they suffer from TS. In the *King's Speech*, a film based on actual events, one of the unorthodox methods therapist Lionel Logue employed to help King George VI overcome his stammering was to have "Bertie" swear. Logue saw that swearing was not afflicted by stammering, and he had the king swear to himself during a sentence when a stammering fit was about to come on. Logue was not an accredited therapist, but he saw that there was a neurological link between swearing and speech patterns.

For a further scientific explanation of swearing, TS, and the Neuro-Pyscho-Social (NPS) theory of cursing, I would highly recommend Jay's *Why We Curse* as an introduction into the psycholinguistic study of swearing. In the words of the preeminent art historian Erwin Panofsky on why he chose not to analyze the work of the painter Hieronymus Bosch, "This, too high for my wit, I prefer to omit."

The term "street talk" is also often used as a synonym for plain speaking. More often than not, it is slang, but it can also be a reference to the unvarnished truth. The term has also been opted by groups in advertising campaigns as an indication of being savvy. There is even an investing firm, StreetTalk, with StreetTalk Advisors who promise to honestly and effectively guide you to investing your money wisely. It also indicates that the speaker is using a hip, up-to-the-minute language. As rich as street language can be, including contributions from the linguistic melting pot that is continually brewing around us, its source is to be found in the creative need to expressive ourselves. "Blow," for cocaine, "bling bling," for jewelry, or "homeslice," for a close friend, are all original ways of defining the same mundane words we use every day. For those who believe that overuse of words devalues them, coiners of street slang would obviously agree. In fact, in many instances, slang is replacing our so-called dirty words: "junk" is a substitute for "balls," "knowledge" is oral sex, and "M10r" is a brilliant stand in for "motherfucker," the 10 in the middle being a replacement for the missing ten letters, "otherfucke." Purely innocent words can be demonized as well. Playing "Good Golly, Miss Molly" on the radio would have no repercussions or garner censure. However, MTV bleeped out the "dancing with molly" line during Miley Cyrus's "We Can't Stop" performance on the 2013 MTV video music awards. (Kanye West was also muted by the MTV censors when he rapped "molly" on the song "Blood on the Leaves.") Molly in this respect is not a woman's name, but is an abbreviation for "molecular" and is a pure form of MDMA (ecstasy).

And for all of the fuss about the media influencing us with the bombardment of swearing, street language would mostly prove be the opposite. The word on the street is taken up by writers to add realism to their work. The wildly popular Stieg Larsson novels or HBO's *The Wire* probably had little or no impact upon the language of those readers and viewers who followed them. On the contrary, *The Wire* is an enlightening study of how people on the street talk. Screenwriter, and former police reporter, David Simon culled from his own investigations to present a realistic portrayal of the turmoil of urban life and of sociopolitical themes. What made his gritty show one of the most critically acclaimed ever made was his scrupulous attention to street talk as an emotional outlet for his characters. We mentioned earlier that the media shapes our language while mirroring it, but swearing on the street transferred to literature or film is more like the old TV show *Candid Camera*, capturing us in the act and impartially playing it back to amuse or embarrass us.

9

IS NOTHING SACRILEGIOUS . . . YET?

"Oh, the Protestants hate the Catholics
And the Catholics hate the Protestants
And the Hindus hate the Moslems
And everybody hates the Jews"
—Tom Lehrer, "National Brotherhood Week"

Practically nothing is sacrilegious, it would appear—unless you resort to a racial slur or the word "cunt." I am not alone in this estimation. Among several authors who understandably point the finger at the former, Richard Dooling in *Blue Streak* agrees that "for centuries, *fuck* was the most objectionable word in the English language, but now *nigger* and *cunt* are probably tied for that distinction, and fuck has long stepped down." Historically, cursing in its original sense—along with blasphemy—was once the most grievous of verbal offenses. Eventually allusions to sexual acts, excretion, and the body parts associated with them became the paradigmatic dirty words. Dooling concurs: "We are on the cusp of taboos, where formerly prohibited terms for sex and excrement are becoming more acceptable and are being replaced by the new unspeakable: racial or ethnic slurs and gender stereotypes."

In conclusion to his comprehensive history of swearing, Geoffrey Hughes agrees that "generally speaking, religious referents and expletives are increasingly regarded as inoffensive, that sexual terms still have much resonance, but that the new area of genuinely potent taboo is race." Currently, as of the beginning of the twenty-first century, the "N-word" has far surpassed the "F-word" and its associates in cussing crime as the single most objectionable word in American English. So, "niggers" or "cunts"—can we get more offensive than that? Of course we can, but let us begin with the former, racism. Studies here and in Great Britain reveal that swear words were more likely to be accepted in films for viewing by younger teenagers when in the context of humorous rather than violent or racially abusive terms.

Melvin Lasky hit upon a significant variable between the present and the recent past with his assessment that "the difference between the nineteenth and the twentieth centuries is that, in the former, the popular words for sex were secret and prohibitive and the rough and ready words of race were open and flagrant. In the latter, and especially in our own times, it is the other way round. Racialist terms are subjected to the code of political correctness and even Mark Twain can't get away with *coon*, even Leo Rosten can't get away with *kike*." Paula Dean was the queen of southern cooking until she was dethroned due to her alleged racism. But returning to Lasky's point about the rough and ready words of race, this lasted right into the twentieth century. The audience that was present at the first production of Jerome Kern's and Oscar Hammerstein's musical *Showboat* in 1927, based on Edna Ferber's caustic play about alcoholism, miscegenation, gambling, and desertion, heard these opening lines:

Niggers all work on de Mississippi,
Niggers all work while de white folk play –
Loadin' up boats wid de bales of cotton,
Gittin' no rest till de Judgement Day.

Since then the lyrics "niggers all work" have been altered to "Negros all work," "black folk all work," "colored folk work," and perhaps the most anesthetizing of all, "Here we all work on the Mississippi." Yes, let's all work and sing together on the Mississippi, happily toten' barges and carryin' bales. Sounds like fun, doesn't it? Of course, Hammerstein was keenly aware of prejudice, bigotry, and the subjugation of fellow human beings, and his original lyric was a well-thought-out prelude to a show with several subplots. Along with segregation and inequality in the South, there was a tale of resilient females struggling to succeed in a male-dominated world. And yet, those opening lyrics can still encroach upon our comfort zone with the visceral immediacy of a kidney punch. John McGlinn's 1988 recording of *Showboat* restored the original lyrics that had been dutifully excised after the original production, but the verity of his project was squeamishly avoided in the Broadway revival of 1994, in which the lines reverted to the more facile "colored folk." After all, it was now supposed to be a musical, and even if it had serious undertones, the overtones were that of a carefully financed contemporary Broadway after a blockbuster hit— and not an insightful or thought-provoking jaunt into reality the way Hammerstein's protégé Stephen Sondheim was to ascribe to and attain throughout his unparalleled work in the theater.

Hollywood was just beginning to talk in 1927, with *The Jazz Singer*, but within the next decade dozens of words were verboten on the screen; "nigger" was not one of them. Melissa Mohr recalls the lesser-known scandal involving *Gone with the Wind*. The squabble over Rhett Butler's use of the atrocious "damn" is now legendary, but there was trouble on the set when the film's black actors refused to say the word "nigger," which had figured prominently in Margaret Mitchell's book. It was only after hundreds of letters poured into David O. Selznick's office that the producer snipped it from the script.

Jews have seemed to bear a particular brunt of this throughout history to the extent that even the word "Jew" has been considered to be derogatory. Reading a news story about the Jews claiming a historic right to Palestine, or listening to an account of the tragedy of the Holocaust that the Jews suffered during World War II, will not raise an eyebrow at the mention of Jews in those contexts. In its singular form, though, saying the word "Jew" can cause some discomfort for many people. When Diane Keaton said, "You're what Granny Hall would call a real Jew" to Woody Allen in *Annie Hall*, it garnered its expected laugh. By casting this dubious aspersion on a Jew, Keaton was a setup for Allen's true intention: to deride those insensitive WASPs for taking such imprecations so cavalierly.

Jack Lynch remarked that while "many people who are comfortable saying *a Christian, a Buddhist,* or *a Muslim* might still say *a Jewish person*, out of conviction that a Jew is a put-down." These people are not without their reasons. Unlike "Christian," "Buddhist," or "Muslim," "Jew" does come with a supply of negative associations. These examples from the OED have served to cause quite a controversy over the years: "to Jew" (usury), "Jew baiting" (harassment), "Jew bail" (insufficient bail). The OED definitions were declaimed as "derogatory, defamatory, and deplorable" in a public lawsuit filed by the Jewish businessman Marcus Schloimovitz, against Clarendon Press in 1969, demanding that the word be dropped from the English language. The case was finally decided four years later in favor of the publisher, the Clarendon Press.

Americans have a notorious lineage of anti-Semitism. Among the more illustrious personages, Nixon was recorded on tape as saying, "The fucking Jews think they rule the world." Hillary Clinton was quoted in the *London Times* for her slip, "Fucking Jew Bastards," and James Baker was overheard saying to Bush senior, "Fuck the Jews. They don't vote for us anyway." The media and the entertainment industry have provided an impetus for linguistic frankness, but the most egregious verbal taboo is now the ethnic or racial epithet. Interestingly, as much as people are caught swearing or joking about the Jews, most of them are still keenly aware not to be heard uttering one word in particular, the "N-word." The hundreds of racial slurs—such as "towelhead," "spic," "wop," "kyke," and "chink," to name but a few—can arouse more ire than a thousand "fucks," but the word "nigger" is by far the most salacious. We have seen that the overuse of words, profane or otherwise, diminishes their effect, but even Lenny Bruce could not mollify racial epithets:

Are there any niggers here tonight? Could you turn on the house lights, please, and could the waiters and waitresses just stop serving, just for a second? And turn off this spot. Now what did he say? "Are there any niggers here tonight?" I know there's one nigger, because I see him back there working. Let's see, there's two niggers. And between those two niggers sits a kyke. And there's another kyke— that's two kykes and three niggers. And there's a spic. Right? Hmm? There's another spic. Ooh, there's a wop; there's a polack; and, oh, a couple of greaseballs. And there's three lace-curtain Irish micks. And there's one, hip, thick, hunky, funky, boogie. Boogie boogie. Mm-hmm. I got three kykes here, do I hear five kykes? I got five kykes, do I hear six spics, I got six spics, do I hear seven niggers? I got seven niggers. Sold American. I pass with seven niggers, six spics, five micks, four kykes, three guineas, and one wop. Well, I was just trying to make a point, and that is that it's the suppression of the word that gives it the power, the violence, the viciousness. Dig: if President Kennedy would just go on television, and say, "I would like to introduce you to all the niggers in my cabinet," and if he'd just say "nigger nigger nigger nigger nigger" to every nigger he saw, "boogie boogie boogie boogie boogie," "nigger nigger nigger nigger nigger" 'til nigger didn't mean anything anymore, then you could never make some six-year-old black kid cry because somebody called him a nigger at school.

As a comedian, Bruce attempted to use humor to eradicate the racial epithet. While it is common knowledge that people of particular ethnicities can tell jokes in public about their own race without fearing the reprisals that others of different races would have visited upon them if they did likewise, that is still in the realm of humor. Outside that jocular realm, however, is a much broader landscape where the words once used in jest will be taken as the denigrating language of racism. As a comedian, Bruce attempted to use humor to eradicate the racial epithet. Louis C.K. took the baton and ran with it in his monologue "Cunt and Nigger."

While Bruce hit upon the critical factor that makes a racial slur what it is—"it's the suppression of the word that gives it the power, the violence, the viciousness"—it is specifically due to the prohibitive nature of the N-word that will not readily allow it to be tamed into superfluity via redundancy or overkill. The mere sound alone insinuates repugnance, whether or not there is the intention to degrade. A striking example is the 1999 case of David Howard, head of the Office of Public Advocate in Washington, DC. Howard used the word "niggardly" in a conversation about administration. Although the word, which is defined as miserly, does not have any racial connotations, Howard realized that staff members present were offended by the word, and he immediately apologized. The rumor that he had used a racial slur instantly spread, and they resulted in such hostility that Howard admitted with great frustration that it so severely compromised his effectiveness as the district's public advocate that he resigned.

Perhaps the sole arena where one can get away with using the actual word is, ironically, among African-Americans. As if they are attempting to suck the evil out of the word, albeit much to the distress of some of their elders, many young black youth casually and defiantly drop it in every-day speech. Rap singers dance with it like snake handlers who have now gained the power over a once-venomous charge. It is also often a badge of identity, when spelled or pronounced "nigga." According to

Edith Folb, in terms of address and identification, its use can "connote affection, playful derision, genuine anger, or mere identification of another black person; used emphatically in conversation. The humorist Dick Gregory penned the book *Nigger* (1964) as his indictment of an oppressive society. He opened the work with a light hearted dedication: Dear Momma—Where ever you are, if you ever hear the word 'nigger' again, remember they are advertising my book." But after 200 pages of this provocative memoir, he poignantly concludes:

And now we're ready to change a system, a system where a white man can destroy a black man with a single word. Nigger.

When we're through, Momma, there won't be any niggers anymore.

Of course, as it is with any other ethnic slur, you better be of that ethnicity to use it. A case in point was the special dispensation granted to a white basketball coach of a mostly black team to use the term just as they did. Perhaps the team viewed it as a form of camaraderie, but the administration and other students took umbrage for violating their taboos, and the coach was fired. Evidently, the offense is not strictly in the word, but from the particular individual who utters it. However widespread the word in question may be, its province is strictly that of a selective group.

And this brings us to what Jack Lynch has called, in his aptly titled book, *The Lexicographer's Dilemma.* Are words that are deemed derogatory or defamatory to be omitted from dictionaries if they are universally found in common speech? He cites Robert Burchfield, editor of the supplementary volumes of the *Oxford English Dictionary*, for his argument that it is the "duty of the lexicographer to record actual usage . . . not to express moral approval or disapproval of usage." Over recent years, further attempts to stifle the lexicographer have manifested themselves in objections railed against *Merriam-Webster's Collegiate Dictionary, Random House Webster's Dictionary, The American Heritage Dictionary,* and *Collins English Dictionary.*

O. J. Simpson's lawyer Johnnie Cochran understood the N-word's volatility all too well, and he attempted to use it to divert the court when he declared that one of the policemen in the case had used the word "nigger." The prosecution immediately protested, knowing very well what Cochran was doing: "If you allow Mr. Cochran to use this word and play the race card, the direction and focus of the case now changes: it is a race case now. . . . It's the filthiest, dirtiest, nastiest word in the English language." In effect, it shows how accurate Lenny Bruce's assessment was. Words have power through suppression. While "nigger" has retained its vile stigma and power, in part through suppression, George Carlin's "heavy seven" have been undermined and devalued through excess, and we as speakers have been anesthetized to their intrinsic vulgarity. I don't know if the group Gangsta Rap was familiar with Bruce's quest to defuse an epithet through overkill, or to actually detonate it, but they were playing a similar game in their song *Nigga, Nigga, Nigga, Nigga, Nigga, Nigga, Nigga* from the 2008 film *Glockumentary*. In just the first verse, the word "nigga" is repeated more than sixty times. The artists here are seemingly making two concurrent statements. On one hand they have taken a word intended to demean, as if capturing the enemy's flag, and are now defiantly waving it as their own. On the other hand, with lyrics such as "why you drink so much beer?" the fact that they are cynically acknowledging very insulting stereotypes railed at them as true shows that they are actually immune to the poison that has been directed at them. Other lyrics include, "why you eat so much chicken?" and "why yo pants gotta sag?" As with the de-sexualizing of "fuck," gangsta rap has forcefully shattered a taboo by proudly invoking it. The artist Matisse and his circle were referred to by critics as *fauves*, or wild beasts, for their divergence from convention. If they were offended, they took the offense by claiming the word Fauvism as their brand of art. Similarly, "nigga" has become a liberating watch cry, which consequently means that it now is a de-fanged snake in the charge of their epithet hurling, bigoted oppressors.

As an aside, the "Glock" in *Glockumentary* is the name of a series of Austrian semiautomatic pistols, which account for about 65 percent of handguns used by United States law enforcement agencies.

Meanwhile, other black Americans have railed against the word. In 2007 the N.A.A.C.P. organized a "funeral" in Detroit for the word "nigger." "Good riddance. Die, n-word," said Kwame Kilpatrick, then the mayor. "We don't want to see you around here no more."

Then there is the lighter side of racism. Not all recordings with that same "parental advisory" sticker for explicit content are created equal. The year 2002 saw the Tony Award go to the "kidult" musical *Avenue Q*, which was something of a grown-up's version of *Sesame Street*, complete with lead-playing puppets. With songs like "The Internet Is For Porn" and "It Sucks to Be Me," *Avenue Q* was a topical recitation of Gen-Xers coming to grips with the onset of adulthood and responsibility. It did so, however, with its tongue solidly in cheek at time, and blatantly sticking out at others. In what may be the most hilarious song about racism ever written—"Everyone's a Little Bit Racist"—we have a Caucasian puppet, a monster puppet, a Japanese woman, and Gary Coleman (played by a black woman) taking part in a self-confessional number about the truth that everyone, indeed, is a little bit racist. The point they try to make in the sweetly tuneful ditty sung by all four is that admitting your ingrained prejudice may be the real first step in eradicating it. The song maintains that everyone is indeed a little bit racist, and if everyone could only admit it and stop being so P.C., maybe we could live in harmony. A little naive, perhaps, and a galaxy away from *Nigga, Nigga, Nigga, Nigga, Nigga, Nigga, Nigga*, but sometimes that's all it takes to set things right.

As with the word "fuck," "cunt" has a lineage that has been written about elsewhere and need not be repeated here. Other sources point to Chaucer as one of the authors to use it in print in *The Miller's Tale*, although as "queynte": "And prively he caught her by the queynte." There was, interestingly enough, a street in thirteenth-century London called Gropecuntlane, and it would take very little imagination to guess what went on there. While the word always had a sexual connotation, in English at least, the consensus is that it did merit a truly pejorative sense until the eighteenth century. Grose was among several lexicographers to include the word in their dictionaries. He spelled it "C**t" and referred to it as "a nasty name for a nasty thing." It goes without saying that former assessment became so great that later dictionaries shunned the word completely, and most continued to do so until the mid-1960s. It does inform us, however, that there may have been many other words already considered too taboo to print that even Grose would not dare print. For example, "fuck" as a primary definition, with or without asterisks, is absent, although it does turn up in other instances such as in the perfectly descriptive phrase "Duck F-ck-r," being "The man who has the care of poultry on board a ship of war." Personally, I dread to imagine what it would have been like to be branded a "duck fucker," save for the fact that the duck fuckers were the ones with the knives. Well, lord love a duck!—or fuck a duck! In either case, "duck" and "fuck" have gone hand in hand for centuries. I have not bothered to figure out why there is a sanctity or damnation of ducks, save for the fact that "duck" rhymes with "fuck." For any other reason, I would caution you to steer clear of ducks.

One reason that the word "cunt' may still shock with greater intensity than "fuck" is exactly what has diminished "fuck's" volatility, and that is the limitation of "cunt's" flexibility. (And, it doesn't rhyme with duck.) The word is used exclusively as a noun, whether it is in reference to the pudendum itself or as a person. We don't have "cunting computers," nor do we say that winning an Oscar was "cunting easy!" Does anyone say, "Cunt you, you mothercunter!" Then there is the issue of gender. "Cunt" is clearly one of those words used by men to subjugate and demean the opposite sex—as well as other men they wish to deem inferior. It is a control word, and its connotation is so rigidly entrenched in our psyches that the politically correct male would rather swallow a box of finishing nails before saying it aloud in mixed company. Like the ethnic slur that denigrates another human being due to his race, "cunt" is still viewed as a sexual slur that debases women. Ruth Wajnryb points to the locus of power in patriarchal societies as an explanation of why the male ego has felt threatened by women and, in turn, why males defend themselves by attacking a female's quintessence: "Given that [the power] is held by males and given that it falls within their capacity to adopt as their most abusive term the word denotatively refers to the most intimate female place, this is what they have done."

Whether or not one agrees that we live in a society that once was very strongly a patriarchal one, slurs rooted in male genitalia are far less offensive than female: dick, ball buster, cocksucker. Moreover, perhaps because of the words' overuse, women as well as men will use these terms: "You are such a dick" or "Stop breaking balls." While these phrases may hardly be as common in a woman's arsenal of swears as in a man's, these expressions are casual. That is to say that a woman would not call someone a "cunt" except in an extreme case—as "fightin' words." This should come as no surprise, since even in polite conversation a woman may affectionately refer to another as "one of the guys," whereas a man would be more apt to slug another if he was called a "gal." We may have come a long way from the patriarchal society we once had, and we often think twice before referring to "every man" and opt for "every man and woman," but the residue of "maleness" still lingers in our speech.

Lenny Bruce, George Carlin, and many other men have taken on a cavalcade of four-letter words in the hope of taming them, but when it comes to the word "cunt," the ball seems to be in the women's court. Eve Ensler christened Valentine's Day "V-Day," although not for St. Valentine but for "vagina," the subject of her off-Broadway play, *The Vagina Monologues*. Working on the premise that overuse will diminish the shock value of the word, Ensler invited the audience to repeat the word "cunt" out loud along with her. By far the greatest paean to the "anatomical jewel," as she calls it, is Inga Muscio's unambiguously titled *Cunt: A Declaration of Independence*. Over the course of nearly 400 pages, she extols the word's origins and declares that women should resurrect it from the pit of male negativity and restore it to its place of honor as a noble word: "Based on the criteria that 'cunt' can be neither co-opted nor spin-doctored into having a negative meaning, venerable history or not, it's ours to do with what we want. And, thanks to the versatility and user-friendliness of the English language, 'cunt' can be used as an all-new, woman-centered, cuntlovin' noun, adjective or verb."

In effect, Muscio has attempted to bring out into the open and glorify what has been shamefully concealed, and she concludes her book with a heartening "Have a nice, cuntlovin' day." Sarah Silverman is known quite well for her verbal assaults and potty-mouth songs and monologues that deal with almost everything from poop to "porn store blowholes," and she clearly has no intention to lionize the word. "Would You Like to See My Pwootheh" may play with it, so to speak, but her song "Cunt" makes no bones about her feelings regarding its use as an invective. She sings, "If you're selfish and you're thoughtless/ and broken and you're heartless/ you're probably not a diva, but a cunt." She then repeats the last word over 60 times to end the little ditty.

Wajnryb, who devotes an entire chapter—"A Cunt of a Word"—to the word would, like so many of us, welcome a time when it is deprived of its nastiness. Nevertheless, she admits that such a time is a long way off: "It remains an extreme term of abuse, carrying the meanings of evil, unfair, devious, and of the lowest nature." Of course, we should also bear in mind that she is Australian, and their approach, like those of other English-speaking countries, can be markedly different in its tenor than that in the United States.

Sadly, the battle for gentility will be one against very heavy odds. As Hughes pointed out, Henley and Farmer listed approximately 700 synonyms for "cunt" and "pudendum" under the euphemistic heading "Monosyllable," thereby making it the single most referenced definition in the entire seven-volume opus. Meanwhile, slang pundit Jonathon Green has compiled some 2,600 words for genitalia over the ages, and has even created a database in the form of a timeline.

To reiterate a matter we touched upon earlier, the growth of "profanity," in the strictest sense of a sacred word used to secular ends, was a reaction to the suppressing mores of the deeply entrenched Puritan ethic in America. Swearing can be viewed as an act of rebellion, a challenge to an established order. Its proponents were rebelling against the idea that words could be dirty or inflammatory, and boldly speaking them freely and without shame was an attempt to remove the taboo that had been placed upon them. Idealistically, it is not inconceivable to think that one day the C-word and the N-word will not strike the same tenor of abhorrence that they do. "Fuck" was once a linguistic no-no in public, and in more genteel times it was credible to assume that it was restricted to battlefields and barrooms—but it clearly wasn't. It has been a short road since the word "damn" was delivered in film to an era when "fuck" and its variants were mentioned over 250 times in the film *Pulp Fiction* (which, given the running time, is approximately two a minute. Lynch has gone on to say, "It may seem that our culture has reached the point at which it's impossible to be offended by words."

This will not stop the language police and the politically correct from continuing to try to stifle "doin' what comes so naturally" to us. Dooling marvelously encapsulates our inherent need to swear: "If you took two human beings, blinded them, deafened them, cut off their limbs, stuffed rags in their mouths, stacked them on top of each other, and kept them alive by intravenous feeding, they eventually would develop a language, probably one based upon the syntax of the nervous system, a sort of palpable dermographia, whereby ideas and emotions would be conveyed tactilely by way of epidermal braille. Rest assured, they would communicate, somehow."

What Dooling has expressly put his finger on is our need to communicate. Language is at its most open in recent history, and we are subsequently voicing our fears, angers, passions, and joys with unbounded freedom. If you recall the maxim from the 1960s, "Let it all hang out," we have apparently done just that to a great extent. Rivaling the extent to which we have given vent to our matrix of emotions, is the divergent vocabulary we have embraced to embody that hodgepodge of emotions. Early on we saw that Ashley Montagu believed that the trend for the future use of four-letter words was unpromising. To reiterate, he maintained that with "the relaxation of the taboos in print, it is not long before they lose their power to frighten and annoy and are employed in open speech." He ventured that when the words become acceptable Standard English, "the power that they enjoyed in their pariah period will gradually become attenuated, and, thus weakened, the four-letter words may disappear entirely from the swearer's vocabulary and vanish into husks and the formless ruin of oblivion." Twenty-five years later, Pareles voiced a similar opinion, "Deploying the f-bomb also defuses it; give or take a few copycats in the months to come, it's going to sound about as potent as a popgun." Diffused or as potent as a pop gun, if anything, Americans are spouting more four-letter words than ever, and the husks and formless ruin of oblivion do not appear to be lurking around my corner. To keep the impact of your verbal potency, it would be wise to heed the words of Tristram Shandy's father: "A wise and just man, however, would always endeavour to proportion the vent given to these humours, not only to the degree of stirring within himself, but the size and ill intent of the offence upon which they fall."

Although our focus here has been on swearing in English, and particularly American English, it must be admitted that swearing is a universal phenomenon. Renatus Hartogs proposed: "If it did not exist, it would probably have to be invented in order to permit humans a psychologically suitable vehicle for the ventilation of fury and despair, the elimination of anger and aggression, the expression of rebellion, and the suppression of fears." And let us not forget the good-old dirty joke. Nevertheless, even as four-letter words permeate our language in our everyday speech, becoming more and more a part of our cultural identity, there will always be those individuals and groups seeking some self-defined and self-imposed purity lurking in the shadows and ready to pounce on their would-be offenders. Censorship is like the troll under the bridge waiting in the dark for the unsuspecting traveler who believes that all is clear and he is free to pass. Just as "good" and "evil" are relative terms that betray chameleon-like existences, so, too, the use of the words "good" and "bad" to characterize language is an arbitrary assessment of the phrases that pass our lips. Those attempting to regulate speech clearly have their definition of "good" language, but their ability to silence those who employ "bad" language will be about as successful as anyone would be attempting to vanquish what is presumptively "evil." This has not prevented them from trying their damnedest to cleanse everyone's speech on their terms.

Ironically, those salty, blue words have undeniably engendered a rich mantle of speech that even its detractors must despairingly acknowledge. The nineteenth-century philologist Richard Trench lamented, "It is a melancholy thing to observe how much richer is every vocabulary in words that set forth sins, than those that set forth graces." In the unimaginable sanitized world of language where only the assumed "good" words abided, Rilke's trepidations would undoubtedly be ours too: "If my devils are to leave me, I am afraid my angels will take flight as well."

APPENDIX

BIRD IS THE WORD

"It's a one-finger salute."
—George W. Bush, placing his middle finger
to his brow before a recorded speech

Nixon did it—and there is no surprise there—and so did Kennedy. Most notably Nelson Rockefeller appeared on the cover of the *New York Post* "flipping off" a heckler, and George W. Bush has been caught numerous times on tape grinning broadly and flashing his favorite "one-finger salute." Just as every nation has its own array of verbal assaults, so do all of them have gestures to let your fingers do the talking. In the United States, the ubiquitous raised middle finger is our call to arms. Unlike swearing, which is based upon actual words with specific meanings, gestures are arbitrary and almost entirely symbolic. Jerry Seinfeld waggishly played with this in an episode of *Seinfeld* titled "The Robbery":

It seems like such an … arbitrary, ridiculous thing to just pick a finger and you show it to the person. It's a finger, what does it mean? Someone shows me one of their fingers and I'm supposed to feel bad. Is that the way it's supposed to work? I mean, you could just give someone the toe, really, couldn't you? I would feel worse if I got the toe, than if I got the finger 'Cause it's not easy to give someone the toe.

Historically, "the bird," as it is affectionately known, dates back to a passage in *The Clouds* by Aristophanes, but it was in ancient Rome, where it was called the *digitus impudicus*, or the "impudent finger," that the finger rose to the fore. In an epigram of the first century poet Martial, he "points his finger, and the insulting one at that, towards Alcon, Dasius and Symmachus." When Emperor Caligula offered his extended middle finger, rather than his hand, for his subjects to kiss, observers found the act scandalous and offensive. The gesture became so abhorrent that Augustus Caesar banished an actor from Italy for giving the finger to an audience member who hissed at the actor during a performance. Clearly the reference is phallic, and this gesture went hand in hand with the "forearm jerk," in which a clenched fist is jerked forcibly upward while the other hand is slapped down in the bend of the elbow. The latter is still common throughout Europe, but the United States seems to have an exclusive hold on the former.

Without question, the bird is our most common insulting gesture. The bird flies everywhere, from schoolyards to the Oval Office. As Ira Robbins contends, though:

Despite its ubiquity, however, a number of recent cases demonstrate that those who use the middle finger in public run the risk of being stopped, arrested, prosecuted, fined, and even incarcerated under disorderly conduct or breach-of-peace statutes and ordinances. . . . Although most convictions are ultimately overturned on appeal, the pursuit of criminal sanctions for use of the middle finger infringes on First Amendment rights, violates fundamental principles of criminal justice, wastes valuable judicial resources, and defies good sense.

The courts are continually faced with arrest cases where police arrest obstreperous individuals for disturbing the peace or for using "fighting words" in conjunction with lewd gestures, but the decisions almost always conclude that flipping someone off does not support a disorderly conduct conviction, even when it is directed toward a police officer. Robbins notes that this approach "allows individuals to criticize the police in a nonviolent way without risking arrest and prosecution." And, like swearing, the bird has been testing the challenging media watchdogs. One would expect to find it in film, but it has even made its way to commercial TV in episodes of *NYPD Blue*. If there is any question as to whether kids know the meaning of the bird, you can go back as far as April 1974 when the cover of *MAD Magazine* featured a drawing of a hand with the middle finger extended and the words "The Number One Ecch Magazine." No one took the magazine to court, but many distributors and newsstands refused to distribute the issue and the publisher received hundreds of complaints. The magazine is now a prized collector's item—as of this writing selling for $29.99 on eBay.

Recall we mentioned that your sudden emotional swearing after stubbing your toe is basically an instinctive vocal reflex and not a direct verbal statement;—flipping someone off is often just as unpremeditated. Cut in front a New Yorker on the Long Island Expressway during Friday night rush hour, and see what he does. Since you cannot hear him, his instinctive response will most likely be a raised digit. Road rage may be the chief catalyst for inspiring the "highway salute," but giving the premeditated finger is a sign of disapproval that takes many forms. Rowan and Martin's long-running comedy television program *Laugh-In* was known for treading the fine-censorship line. Every week it presented bikini-clad—or just-clad—go-go dancers and characters with names such as Fred Farkel, General Bull Right, and Tyrone F. Horneigh (pronounced hor-NIGH to appease the censors), along with a fey sports announcer named Big Al, and delivered suggestive lines like "Want a Walnetto?" and "You bet your sweet bippy!" The award-winning comedy cavalcade titillated audiences for nearly ten years with sly double entendre and ribald humor, but a highlight of every episode was "The Flying Fickle Finger of Fate Award," saluting actual dubious achievements by the government, celebrities, or other public figures who committed bone-headed deeds. With alliterative three "Fs," and an oversized, outstretched pointing finger atop a square base, the gilt trophy left few audience members guessing what was really intended. Actions may speak louder than words, but when the flying fickle finger of fate was aimed at a miscreant, it needed no words.

The bird is used to convey a wide range of emotions, and even the manner in which one delivers it is equally diverse. The amusing little volume *Field Guide to the North American Bird* sets forth step-by-step illustrations for more than fifty variations, including the "Peel the Banana," the "Corkscrew," and the "Fly Fisherman." What makes the bird handy is that it can be used to cover great distances and penetrate realms that the good-old "fuck you" cannot. As Jay says, "Speaker anonymity allows one to disrespect people without recourse or retaliation. The opposing team's pitcher may not be able to hear you shouting among thousands of other booing fans, but he sure as hell can see that single digit waving at him. Similarly, just as you might have seen on the Long Island Expressway, you may not hear the stream of four-letter words, but you will see that impudent digit swirling in your rearview mirror. It's also valuable when your boss tells you to quit goofing off and get back to work, and you can give him that one-gun salute as he turns his back. Yes, when words fail, there is always the finger. It can speak volumes in silence. Meanwhile, our ever-cautious *New York Times* did cross a line in the following clue in the June 30, 2012 crossword puzzle: Bird. If you guessed "onefingersalute" as the answer, you would be correct.

To sum up, what do actresses Britney Spears, Avril Lavigne, Charlize Theron, Cameron Diaz, Jodie Foster, and Queen Latifah have in common? Middle digit raised high, they have all been caught on camera in a "no-comment" comment to the ladies and gentlemen photographers of the press. It is also the recourse of the sore loser. Anthony Weiner lived up to his name when he awarded the single-digit to an NBC reporter after losing in the New York City mayoral primary. One would almost think that the gesture was especially invented to flip-off prying paparazzi, but a short tour of images on Google will show that giving the finger is something the average individual, from toddler to octogenarian, can do just as capably as celebrities. And, to paraphrase the words of the young lad to Shoeless Joe Jackson for taking part in the "Black Sox" scandal helping to fix the 1919 World Series, "Say it ain't so, Mr. Rogers." Yes, even on one beautiful day in the neighborhood, poor Fred was caught on videotape raising both hands and doing a *double*-digit salute.

However you do it—blatantly or discreetly—flipping the bird is a tried and true silent form of speech that can well fill the gap for a hearty "fuck you" when the latter is unavailable. In concert with its verbal cousin, however, it is a cathartic match that can't be topped. Perhaps the most sacrilegious, yet wickedly funny, example of this is a scene from *The Book of Mormon*, where nearly a dozen Ugandans, beset by war, poverty, famine, the rape of babies, and AIDs, find cathartic release in vigorously raising their middle fingers to the sky while singing "Hasa Diga Eebowai," which is later translated as "Fuck you, God." Let us return to the beginning of our jaunt, when I mentioned that Stephen Sondheim had hope to be the first Broadway lyricist to use the word "fuck" in a song. In the fifty-plus years since *West Side Story*, the expletive is not only fully accepted in the theater, but roundly applauded. Mr. Sondheim, though a recognized giant of musical theater, has never had a play of his run more than a thousand performances on Broadway. More than having passed that Broadway milestone, *The Book of Mormon* has had tickets for choice performances running up to $500 a seat. Clearly, the raucous little play had its finger on the pulse of the theater-going public, and that pulse hardly skips a beat, today, when one of the characters exclaims, "Jesus called me a dick!"

But one need not be so obvious to get the point across. In the first episode of season three of PBS's *Sherlock!*, Watson is at work in his doctor's office and Holmes is going about his own business at 221B Baker Street. Watson is angry with his old friend for faking his death, and we see the good doctor first raise his middle finger as he slips on a rubber glove. Shoot to Holmes' study where Mrs. Hudson asks what Watson said to Holmes upon learning of his return. Holmes begins to sound out "fff...," and we immediately shift back to Watson as he tells a patient to "Cough!" (Sound those out together if you don't catch the humor immediately.) "Oh dear," says Mrs. Hudson.

In closing, for all of the trivia fans out there, astronomer Galileo Galilei's middle finger has been meticulously preserved and can be viewed today at the Museo Galileo in Florence, for eight euros. The digit was plucked from his dead body by a souvenir-hunter named Anton Francesco Gori in 1737 when Gori detached the finger while moving the body from a storage closet to a nearby chapel. For a great man who was tried by the Inquisition, found "vehemently suspect of heresy," forced to recant, and who spent the rest of his life under house arrest, isn't it fitting that Galileo is still flipping the bird to the Catholic Church for condemning him for his theory of heliocentrism?

And, if you are not able to confront your adversary face to face, there is always the computer keyboard. Let your fingers do the talking:

```
........................./'¯/)
......................,/¯../ /
...................../..../ /
.............../'¯/'...'/'¯¯`·¸
............/'/.../..../...../¨¯\
..........('(...´(..´......,~/'...')
...........\.................\/..../
............”...\............. _.·´
.............\.............(
.............\..............\
```

ACKNOWLEDGMENTS

I would like to thank Kurt Volkan for his enthusiasm, as well as for his careful editing and invaluable suggestions in seeing this book to its conclusion. I also owe my gratitude to Reinhold "Rey" Aman for taking the time to review the manuscript. My thanks also go out to Keith Allan for sharing his wisdom and fascinating insights on the state of language today. I also cannot express my appreciation enough to lexicographer extraordinaire Jonathon Green for vetting the manuscript and offering what he would modestly call his "ten penn'orth."

Finally, I would like to thank my family for their support, and especially to my wife, Valdina, and my son, Tristan, for inspiring me in more ways than they know …

NOTES

All citations are preceded by the last few words of the sentence they are pertaining to. (And, as it is with the ever-changing English language, so, too, does the Internet have its quirks; which is to say that while all of the links cited below at the time of this writing were valid, some may have swerved off the superhighway and into the ditch of cyber oblivion. The books still work, however.)

13: "Gee, Officer Krupke—Fuck you!" Sondheim, Stephen. (2011) *Finishing the Hat.* New York: Knopf, 51

15: ... and more open explicit means of communication." Jay, Timothy. (1996) *What to Do When Your Students Talk Dirty*, San Jose, California: Resource Publications, 125.

16: ... the dining room table no longer seem to rebuke it. Jay, Timothy. (1992) *Cursing in America.* Philadelphia: John Benjamins Publishing Co., 13

16: ... 'please' and 'thank you.'" Smerconish, Michael. http://www.philly. com/philly/news/20131124_The_Pulse__The_word_that_s_bleeping_ everywhere.html#PBWEjUfmkI8b333M.99

17: "The monarch reigns over language." Sagarin, Edward. (1962) *The Anatomy of Dirty Words.* New York: Lyle Stuart, 137

17: ... sometimes even on formal occasions." Pareles, John. "From Cee Lo Green to Pink, Speaking the Unspeakable," *New York Times*, 3/16/11

17: ... the emotional needs of the speaker." Jay, Timothy. (1999) *Why We Curse: A Neuro-Psycho-Social Theory of Speech.* Philadelphia: John Benjamins Publishing Company, 9

18: ... are employed in open speech." Montagu, Ashley. (1967) *The Anatomy of Swearing.* New York: Macmillan, 320

19: ... over the roofs of the world." Whitman, Walt. "Song of Myself." *Leaves of Grass*

20: ... catharsis, aggression, and social connection. Wajnryb, Ruth. (2005) *Expletive Deleted $&#@*!: A Good Look at Bad Language.* New York: Free Press, 24

20: ... which is to say, subcortically. Pinker, Steven. (1994) *The Language Instinct.* New York: William Morrow and Company, 334

21: ... It is Saturnalian defiance of Destiny." Graves, Robert. (2009.ed) *Lars Porsena: On the Future of Swearing.* London: One World Classics, 30

21: ... All who remain silent are dyspeptic." Nietzsche, Frederick. (n.d.) *Ecce Homo* (trans. Clifton Fadiman). New York: Modern Library, 14

21: ... because then I vented a spleen here." Dowd, Maureen. 1990. "The Language Thing." *New York Times*: http://query.nytimes.com/gst/fullpage.html?res=9C0CE3DB1038F93AA15754C0A966958260&pagewanted=2

22: ... are forbidden because they are emotive." Bryson, Bill. (1990) *The Mother Tongue: English & How It Got That Way.* New York: William Morrow, 218

23: ... imprecation is sonofabitch or motherfucker." Crystal, David. (1995) *The Cambridge Encyclopedia of the English Language.* Cambridge: Cambridge University Press, 173

24: ... with the memorable phrase. http://www.youtube.com/watch?v=PSEYXWmEse8

25: ... *or over radio, or on television."* Sagarin, 31

25: ... or its variations at least 100 times. http://en.wikipedia.org/wiki/List_of_films_that_most_frequently_use_the_word_%22fuck%22

28: ... have at least one tattoo. http://www.borntoride.com/new/wordpress/2009/05/11/tattoo-facts-statistics/

29: ... when it was published." Frost, Vicky. *BBC Radio 3's Wuthering Heights to turn the airwaves blue.* http://www.guardian.co.uk/tv-and-radio/2011/mar/22/bbc-radio-3-wuthering-heights

29: Allan, Keith and Burridge, Kate. (2006) *Forbidden Words.* Cambridge:

Cambridge University Press, 109.

31: ... for their efforts in establishing a no-cussing policy. Severson, Kim. "Trying to Hold Down Blue Language on a Red Letter Day." *The New York Times*. February 13, 2011; National section, 18

31: ... cleaning up their vocabulary. O'Conner, James V. (2000) *Cuss Control*. New York: Three Rivers Press, 1

32: ... in New York's Greenwich Village. Sanders published an account of life in the Village in his 2011 *Fug You: An Informal History of the Peace Eye Bookstore, the Fuck You Press, the Fugs, and Counterculture in the Lower East Side*.

35: ... How to Talk Dirty and Influence People. Bruce, Lenny. (1963) *How to Talk Dirty and Influence People*. Chicago: Playboy Press, 152

36: ... **but dirty to the Latins!**" *The Carnegie Hall Concert*, 1961

36: ... and must be seen." Bruce, ibid., 202

36: ... is particularly diabolical or revolting." McEnery, Tony. (2006) *Swearing in English: Bad language, purity and power from 1586 to the present*. London and New York: Routledge, 118

36: ... fuck the government.'" cited in the film *Fuck: A Documentary*, 2006

38: ... the story of a free speech martyr." both ibid.

42: ... at their word that there are 126. http://www.youtube.com/watch?v=J3dockXbZM8

43: ... "motherfucker" – 1 Hunt, M. and Maloney, Allison. *The Joy of Swearing*. London. Michael O'Mara Books Limited, page 37

43: ... a whopping $95,225,000." http://www.thewvsr.com/deadwood.htm

45: ... She questioned my ancestry." cited in Flexner, Stuart Berg. (1982) *Listening to America: An Illustrated history of Words and Phrases from Our Lively and Splendid Past*. New York: Simon & Schuster, 50-51

46: ... should be working to eradicate." http://www.tmz.com/2011/04/13/kobe-bryant-gay-slur-human-rights-campaign-gay-and-lesbian-lakers-slur-disgrace/

47: ... bodily functions in non-clinical ways. http://en.wikipedia.org/wiki/Esperanto_profanity

48: ... can almost always be used nonliterally," Mohr, Melissa. (2013) *Holy Shit: A Brief History of Swearing*. London. Oxford, 6

49: ... In American English, "fuck" stands alone. see Hughes, G. (1998) *Swearing: A Social History of Foul Language, Oaths, and Profanity in English*. New York: Penguin, 31

49: ... rugs or bad haircuts here. In fact, I have a book called *Sod Calm and Get Angry*—a title that would baffle most Americans. And so, for the U.S. market, the title was changed to *Screw Calm and Get Angry*.

49: ... of the word's usage, *The F Word* by Jesse Sheidlower. Sheidlower, Jesse. (1995) *The F Word*. New York: Random House

50: ... Like I'm talking to a fucking wall." cited in Wajnryb, 26

52: ... all wind up sounding like Yosemite Sam. http://en.wikipedia.org/wiki/Deadwood_%28TV_series%29#Use_of_profanity

52: ... becomes increasingly acceptable. Smerconish, Michael. Op. cit.

53: ... we turn to this salty morsel: cited in Hunt, page 159

53: ... more pleasure than anything else." Bryson, Bill. (1990), 215

54: ... and not literal sexual denotation." Jay, Timothy. (2009) "Do Offensive Words Harm People?" *Public Policy, and Law*, Vol. 15, No. 2, 92 and Fairman, C. (2007). "Fuck." *Cardozo Law Review*, 28, 1171

54: ... by articulating 'gack' or 'krot.'" Crystal, 251

54: ... and, of course, "fuck." ibid.

54: ... such phrases are literally nonsense." Ibid. 173

55: ... a more violent form of BLOODY. Farmer, John S. and Henley, W. E. (1893) *A Dictionary of Slang and Its Analogues*. Vol. III, 80f.

55: ... they had been previously unprinted. Sheidlower, xxix

55: ... and John Dos Passos (... a fucking shame) Ibid., 145

56: "acts performed on the passive female." Wajnryb, 45

56: ... "Fuck! That's a big dog!" (exclamation) from *Macquerie Learner's Dictionary*, cited in Wajnryb, 42 The online Urban Dictionary also elaborates on the nonsexual use of fuck:

> Fraud ...I got fucked at the used car lot.
> Dismay ...ahhh fuck it.

Trouble ...I guess I'm really fucked now.

Aggression ...Don't fuck with me buddy.

Difficulty ...I don't understand this fucking question.

Inquiry ... Who the fuck was that?

Dissatisfaction ...I don't like what the fuck is going on here.

Incompetence ...He's a fuckup. http://www.urbandictionary. com/define.php?term=fuck

57: ... "Aren't they all?" Jay, (1992), 11

58: ... (Christians should not use profanity)." Jay, Timothy. (2005) "American Women: Their Cursing Habits and Religiosity" in *Gender and the Language of Religion*, edited by Jule, Allyson. Hampshire: Palgrave MacMillan, 63

58: ... are ripe for His judgment." Patton, Michael, C. (2007) *Taking the Lord's Name in Vain: What Does It Really Mean?* http://www.reclaimingthemind. org/blog/2007/06/what-does-it-really-mean-to-take-the-lords-name-in-vein/

58: ... you will be blessed." ibid.

58: ... to oath-making and breaking. Mohr, passim

59: ... backcountry brides were in a similar state. cited in Bryson, Bill. (1994) *Made in America: An informal History of the English Language in the United States*. New York: HarperCollins, 306

59: ... sensitive about terms related to sex." ibid. 307

60: ... often seems to "do dirt" on love." from the introduction to Sagarin, 10

60: ... the freewheeling search for self." Hartogs, 24

61: ... without consciousness of its sexual denotation." Legman, g. (1975) *No Laughing Matter*. New York: Bell, 698

61: ... especially "prayers of imprecation" Partridge, E. (1983 ed.) *Origins*. New York: Greenwich House, 136

62: ... Middle English from the Latin *coruptus*. Partridge, Eric. *Origins: A Short Etymological Dictionary of Modern English*. Greenwich House: New York, 136

62: ... its specific meaning was to "damn." Hughes, 7

63: … a malediction hurled at them. Montagu, 8

63: (Your mother's pussy has teeth). http://apocryph.org/2006/08/06/best_arabic_insults/

63: … "The definitive pissed off anthem of our times." http://www.youtube.com/watch?v=NLRNwYhVfWs: "The definitive pissed-off anthem of our times"

64: … of a Rodgers and Hammerstein show." Brantley, Ben. (3/25/11) "Missionary Men with Confidence of Sunshine." *The New York Times.* http://theater.nytimes.com/2011/03/25/theater/reviews/the-book-of-mormon-at-eugene-oneill-theater-review.html?hpw

66: … with the listener-speaker relationship." Jay (1992), 13

66: … (a play in shooting marbles). Cassidy, Frederic G., chief editor. (1991). *Dictionary of American Regional English*, vol. II. Cambridge (Mass.): Belknap Press, 597

66: … reaction of the listener. Jay elaborates on this (1992), 12ff

67: … and even smartness…" cited in Sagarin, 168

67: … measured once per hour. http://www.theatlantic.com/technology/archive/2012/08/how-america-swears-heres-a-heatmap-tracking-twitter-profanity/261438/#.UDa4zcvrmUd.facebook

67: … words lack its flexibility. Smerconish, Michael. Op. cit.

67: … actually has no brewery." http://www.huffingtonpost.com/2010/03/31/fing-hell-europes-new-bee_n_519971.html

70: … bombardments and sudden panics." Graves, 30-31

71: … from his childhood were foul and disgusting." Read, Allen Walker. "An Obscenity Symbol." *American Speech*, vol. 9; no. 4 December 1934, 275

71: … this would seem appropriate." Wajnryb, 141

71: … though not as often as in the past." Mencken, H.L. (1936) *The American Language*. New York: Knopf, 34

71: … 'at off in the 'ouse of God, cunt!" Fussell, Paul. (1989) *Wartime: Understanding and Behavior in the Second World War*. New York: Oxford University Press, 94

71: … of urgency and danger. cited in Mencken, 315

72: ... out on the fucken bed, and had sexual intercourse. cited in Legman, 698

73: ... blank blank blank fuck." Mohr, 227

73: ... evident in the wartime hit *Bloomer Girl.* see Stempel, Larry. (2010) *Showtime: A History of Musical Theater.* New York: W. W. Norton & Co. 316f. for more on this.

75: ... whereas euphemism is a sedative." cited in Sagarin, 115

76: ... "I never learned no Latin." Graves, 19

77: ... the heroism of ordinary Americans at war." www. chicagotribune.com/news/columnists/chi-0411170273nov17,1,3729748. column?coll=chinews-col

77: ... prime-time broadcast hours." ibid.

77: ... with another thrilling blockbuster: *Return to Mayberry.* www. usatoday.com/life/television/news/2004-11-11-private-ryan_x.htm

82: ... would obscure even the darkness of hell!" (March 31, 1930). "Decency Squabble." *Time Magazine.* http://www.time.com/time/magazine/ article/0,9171,738937-1,00.html

82: ... and caused fifteen suicides. Bryson (1994), 315

82: ... I find, however, that you have in looking for them." cited in Read, 271

83: ... in his incisive *Four-Letter Word Games.* Hartogs, Renatus and Fantel, Hans. (1968) *Four-Letter Word Games.* New York: Dell, 7ff

83: ... for the most part, seemed subdued." ibid., 8

84: ... and respectable, prim and prurient." ibid., 11

84: ... "directness over convention." Battistella, Edwin L. (2007) *Bad Language.* New York: Oxford, 77

85: ... That's not very appealing to the public." http://www.aolnews. com/2010/06/08/obamas-swearing-nothing-new-for-presidents/

86: ... IMPEACH THE [EXPLETIVE DELETED]! Lynch, Jack. (2009) *The Lexicographer's Dilemma.* New York: Walker publishing Co., 244

86: ... It's not funny after a while" Nixon tapes, 4/27/71

86: ... did you do any fornicating this weekend?" http://www.

politicsdaily.com/2010/03/26/f-bombs-in-the-white-house-joe-biden-has-lots-of-company/

86: ... which was itself a euphemism at one time. ibid.

86: ... not a particularly holy site for Mr. Gorka. http://politicalticker.blogs.cnn.com/2012/07/31/romney-aide-loses-cool-curses-at-press-in-poland/?hpt=hp_bn3

87: ... since pantyhose ruined finger-fucking." above examples cited in *Fuck: The Documentary*

87: ... has yet contributed to literature." Mencken, H.L. (1918) *Damn! A Book of Calumny*. New York: Philip Goodman, 20

88: ... that "dick and dickhead" were not. http://www.bloomberg.com/news/2010-07-13/fcc-fleeting-expletive-policy-struck-down-by-u-s-appeals-court-as-vague.html

90: ... to exchange oaths instead of blows." Dooling, Richard. (1996) *Blue Streak: Swearing, Free Speech, and Sexual Harassment*. New York: Random House 8

90: ... and telling him, "Go fuck yourself." http://www.eonline.com/news/395669/taylor-swift-steps-out-in-wake-of-her-tina-fey-and-amy-poehler-special-place-in-hell-comment

91: ... in the same country in the same century." Bryson (1994), 313

92: ... everybody knows the meaning of." cited in Bryson, ibid.

92: ... against harsh or profane language." then editor Allan M. Siegal quoted in a letter to Bryson, ibid. 323

92: ... The Times *fails spectacularly*." Allerano, Gustavo. (2/10/08) "So who the *#%&$+ wants to know?" *The Los Angeles Times*. http://articles.latimes.com/2008/feb/10/opinion/op-arellano10

93: ... swear words can be heard on the playground already." Ali, Rubina. (1/24/2011) *The use of profanity in journalism*. http://meyer.media.illinois.edu/500/tag/profanity/

93: ... at the sight of a four-letter word." O'Conner, Claire. (5/18/10) *Rhymes with 'Truck' Profanity in the press: Why is it such a big fucking deal?* http://www.cjr.org/the_student_lounge/rhymes_with_truck.php

94: ... out of touch with the real world." cited in O'Conner. Ibid.

94: … that is germane to the story." cited in O'Conner. Ibid.

94: … in the more conservative *Hartford Courant* http://articles.courant. com/2010-03-24/news/hc-joe-biden-f-bomb.artmar24_1_nice-looking-guy-first-mainstream-african-american-mr-biden

94: … was far removed from those heights." Lasky, Melvin J. (2005) *Profanity, Obscenity & the Media: The Language of Journalism, vol. 2.* Transactions Publishers: New Brunswick, New Jersey, 161

94: … "Well, what *had* he said?" Lasky, 162

95: … was plunged into darkness." ibid.

96: … at least in public." Brantley, Ben. (4/12/11) "A Love Not at a Loss for Words." *The New York Times.* http://theater.nytimes.com/2011/04/12/theater/reviews/the-with-the-hat-by-stephen-adly-guirgis-review.html?adxnnl=1&hpw=&pagewanted=2&adxnnlx=1302624017-Whgvqbv1+/7yNcm6g4La5w

96: … best new plays to come to Broadway in ages." Teachout, Terry. (4/12/11) "Don't Let Its Name Be a Curse." *The Wall Street Journal.* http://online.wsj.com/article/SB10001424052748704529204576256803651095240.html?mod=WSJ_ArtsEnt_LifestyleArtEnt_2

97: … sounded even more explicit." Lasky, 92

97: … nothing to do with religion or the deity." ibib., 93

98: … on its front page as a huge headline. Hoyt, Clark. (11/13/08) "When to quote Those Potty Mouths." *New York Times,* http://www.nytimes.com/2008/07/13/opinion/13pubed.html

99: … was "screw it." *New York Times,* 3/25/13

99: … an exception to stringent *Times* standards." Hoyt, ibid.

99: … so prissy we're out of touch." ibid.

99: … why should we sanitize his expression?" ibid.

99: … Brodkey nixed the offending expletive. http://articles.nydailynews.com/1997-02-21/gossip/18038409_1_magazine-david-leavitt-ad

100: … everything I ever worked for!" Green, Elon. "The Dirty Talk of the Town: Profanity at 'The New Yorker.'" http://www.theawl.com/2011/05/new-yorker-profanity

100: … was still using "blood disease." Mencken, H.L. (1945) *The American Language: Supplement I.* New York: Knopf, 647

100: ... mentioning the words "shit" or "ass." cited in Bryson (1994), 322

100: ... women who have large *derrières*." Mencken. (1936), 307

100: ... and refuse to print the words." Hoyt, ibid.

101: ... to ostentatiously avoid the slang term." Bryson, ibid.

101: ... and in front of company. For a discussion on why "shit" should be a choice word among children, see Hartogs, ibid, 94ff.

103: ... broke their own rules on a regular basis. Jay, http://www.livescience.com/8667-3-kids-learning-swear-earlier.html

104: ... defining speech standards for children." Jay, Timothy. (2009), 97

105: ... "Learning they're taboo words is a later step." http://www.npr.org/templates/story/story.php?storyId=89127830

106: ... When Mich. Hunt itches. Personal correspondence.

106: ... "Thou whoreson, senseless villain" Antipolous in *Comedy of Errors*, IV, iv

106: ... Butchers and villains, bloody cannibals." Queen Margaret in *Henry VI*, pt.III, V, v

106: ... to Shakespeare's conspicuous oaths. Montagu, 136-153

108: ... that's not a wussy there." http://en.wikipedia.org/wiki/Beavis_and_Butt-head

108: ... swearing really takes off between (ages) three and four." For an elaboration on this, as well as specific statistics, see Jay (1992), 17ff.

109: ... one now swears." Montagu, 70

109: ... *Because I bea'nt old enough to swear. Punch*, April 2, 1913

109: ... a sure ticket to adulthood, says Paul Bloom. ibid.

109: ... but they do repeat the words they hear." http://www.livescience.com/8667-3-kids-learning-swear-earlier.html

110: ... You Fudrucker. O'Conner, 185

110: ... They scarcely left to coer their fuds. Jonathon Green. Personal correspondence.

111: ... they can "ship there pants." http://www.youtube.com/watch?v=I03UmJbK0lA

111: ... he feared comfort, satisfaction, joy." Mencken, *Damn!* op. cit. 42

112: ... to impose a $20 fine on public profanity. http://www.usatoday.com/news/nation/story/2012-06-12/middleborough-swearing-fine/55542416/1

113: ... and fuck her too." http://www.youtube.com/watch?v=pc0mxOXbWIU&NR=1&feature=fvwp&oref=http%3A%2F%2Fwww.youtube.com%2Fwatch%3Fv%3DNLRNwYhVfWs&has_verified=1

114: ... and society's sick needs." Legman, 987

114: ... *Lie the fuck down, my darling, and sleep.* Mansbach, Adam. (2011) Go the Fuck to Sleep. New York: Akashic Books

115: ... trying to get your kid to go to sleep." http://www.guardian.co.uk/books/2011/may/17/go-the-fuck-to-sleep-hit

115: ... to get his daughter to go to sleep. http://www.youtube.com/watch?v=OU1ooQUstzI

115: ... could be doing something similar." Žižek, Slavoj. (2006) *The Parallax View.* Cambridge (Mass): the MIT Press, 91

116: ... contained the word "motherfucker." Jay (1992), 34

116: ... to reduce the use of cursing at school." Jay (1996), ix

116: ... that some more polite term be substituted." ibid. 206-207

117: ... in the community of American schools." Robbins, Ira P. "Digitus Impudicus: The Middle Finger and the Law." *University of California, Davis Law Review* Vol. 41:1403: http://crapaganda.com/wp-content/uploads/2010/03/digitus_impudicus_robbins.pdf

117: ... kids in China are starving for it." *Fuck*, ibid.

117: ... *And learn.* Sondheim, Stephen. (1987) *Into the Woods.* From "Children Will Listen."

118: ... because it makes people feel better." http://www.nytimes.com/2012/08/05/movies/q-and-a-chris-rock-is-itching-for-dirty-work.html?src=dayp

119: ... emphatic, percussive four-letter word." Pareles, John. "From Cee Lo Green to Pink, Speaking the Unspeakable," *NYT*, 3/16/11

120: ... a young woman signing the classic song. http://www.youtube.com/watch?v=sv3tadz5Q3o&feature=player_embedded#!

120: ... to shout the forbidden word." Pareles, ibid.

121: ... and driving teenagers to do outlandish things." Blecha, Peter. (2004) *Taboo Tunes: A History of Banned Bands & Censored Songs*. San Francisco: Backbeat Books, 29

121: ... like these jungle beats and rhythms." ibid., 38

121: ... transferred wholesale to the new music." Ibid., 25

121: ... before they go out to hunt heads." Rev. Robert Riblett cited in Blecha, 26

122: ... monotonous, noisy ... and suggestive," ibid., 34

123: ... from "playing risqué music." Nuzum, Eric. (2001) *Parental Advisory: Music Censorship in America*. New York: Harper Perennial, 265

123: ... "sale of harmful material" statute. ibid., 269

124: ... without being charged. ibid., 266

125: ... the police beat up Rodney King?" cited in Nuzum, 279

125: ... *Not* just the right." Blecha, 130

126: ... You can quote me on that." Nuzum, 303

126: ... This is awful." ibid., 304

127: ... *Leavin' on a Jet Plane*. Blecha, 175

127: ... statements posted there by fans. ibid., 176

127: ... and who plays it." ibid., 185

128: ... it's barely an inconvenience." Pareles, op. cit.

130: ... without worrying about retaliation." Jay (1996), 126

130: ... uncontrollable cursing, or coprolalia." Jay (1999), 3

131: ... in 'polite' situations." ibid., 6

131: ... I prefer to omit." Panofsky, Erwin. (1971) *Early Netherlandish Painting*, Vol. I. Cambridge (Mass.): Harvard University Press, 358

133: ... has long stepped down." Dooling, 18

133: ... the paradigmatic dirty words. Lynch, 246

133: ... and gender stereotypes." Dooling, 6

134: ... of genuinely potent taboo is race." Hughes, 279

134: ... than racially abusive terms. Hunt, page 82

134: ... can't get away with *kike*." Lasky, 79

135: ... the producer snipped it from the script. Mohr, 232

136: ... that a Jew is a put-down." Lynch, 247

136: ... "Jew bail" (insufficient bail). all cited in *The Compact Edition of the Oxford English Dictionary*.(1971) Glasgow, et al: Oxford University Press, 1507f.

136: ... from the English language. Lynch, 249

137: ... a thousand 'fucks.' ibid.

137: ... *because somebody called him a nigger at school.* http://en.wikiquote. org/wiki/Lenny_Bruce

138: ... in his monologue "Cunt and Nigger." [http://www.youtube.com/ watch?v=zuLrBLxbLxw]

138: ... the District's Public Advocate that he resigned. [http://www. washingtonpost.com/wp-srv/local/daily/jan99/district27.htm]

138: ... when spelled or pronounced "nigga." Allan, K. and Burridge, K. (2006) *Forbidden Words: Taboo and the Censoring of Language*. Cambridge: Cambridge University Press, 84

139: ... used emphatically in conversation. [Folb, Edith. (1980) *Runnin' Down Some Lines: The Language and Culture of Black Teenagers*. Cambridge (Mass.): Harvard University Press, 248]

139: ... *any niggers anymore.* Gregory, Dick. (1990 edition) *Nigger*. New York: Pocket Books, 209

139: ... and the coach was fired. Allan, K. and Burridge, ibid.

139: ... or disapproval of usage." Lynch, 249

140: ... nastiest word in the English language" cited in Lynch, ibid, 246

141: ... law enforcement agencies. http://en.wikipedia.org/wiki/Glock_pistol

141: "...to see you around here no more." Coates, Ta-Nehisi. http://www. nytimes.com/2013/11/24/opinion/sunday/coates-in-defense-of-a-loaded-word.html?hp&rref=opinion/international&_r=0

141: ...need not be repeated here. Hughes probably gives the most concise etymology, 27

141: ... he caught her by the queynte." Chaucer, Geoffrey. (1396) *The Canterbury Tales*, line 3,276

142: … "a nasty name for a nasty thing." Grose, Francis. (1785) *Classical Dictionary of the Vulgar Tongue.*

143: … this is what they have done." Wajnryb, 80

144: … noun, adjective or verb." Muscio, Inga. (2002) *Cunt: A Declaration of Independence.* New York: Seal Press, 11

144: … over 60 times to end the little ditty. [http://www.youtube.com/watch?v=rNTPzbLPpkk]

144: … and of the lowest nature." Wajnryb, 79

145: … the entire seven-volume opus. Hughes, 13

145: … in the form of a timeline. http://jonathongreen.co.uk/

145: … to be offended by words." Lynch, 245

145: … they would communicate, somehow." Dooling, 160

146: … the formless ruin of oblivion." Montagu, 320

146: … as potent as a popgun." Pareles, ibid.

147: … the suppression of fears." Hartogs, 152

147: … that set forth graces." cited in Dooling, 170

149: … *'Cause it's not easy to give someone the toe.* http://www.seinfeldscripts.com/TheRobbery.htm

149: … Dasius and Symmachus." Martial. *Epigrams*, Book VI:LXX

149: … the actor during a performance. Robbins, ibid.

149: … *and defies good sense."* ibid.

151: … and the "Fly Fisherman." Blank, Adam and Laura. (2004) *Field Guide to the North American Bird.* Berkeley: Ten Speed Press

151: … without recourse or retaliation. Jay (1996), 126

152: … photographers of the press. http://freshpics.blogspot.com/2008/04/celebrity-middle-finger.html

152:…doinga*double*-digitsalute.http://s3-ec.buzzfed.com/static/enhanced/web03/2012/9/28/12/anigif_enhanced-buzz-32537-1348849182-1.gif

INDEX

ABOUT THE AUTHOR

Writer and artist Rob Chirico can attribute his early knowledge of swearing to growing up in New York City. Among other works, he is the author of the popular *Field Guide to Cocktails*. He lives in western Massachusetts.

OTHER TITLES FROM PITCHSTONE

Attack of the Theocrats!
by Sean Faircloth

Candidate Without a Prayer
by Herb Silverman

The Citizen Lobbyist
by Amanda Knief

The Ebony Exodus Project
by Candace R. M. Gorham, LPC

God Bless America
by Karen Stollznow

A Manual for Creating Atheists
by Peter Boghossian

PsychoBible
by Armando Favazza, MD

What You Don't Know about Religion (but Should)
by Ryan T. Cragun

Why Are You Atheists So Angry?
by Greta Christina

Why We Believe in God(s)
by J. Anderson Thomson, Jr., MD, with Clare Aukofer